a *Wee Guide* to

# Macbeth and
# Early Scotland

J. Hall sculp.

MACBETH.

a *Wee Guide* to

# Macbeth and
# Early Scotland

Charles Sinclair

**GOBLINSHEAD**

Musselburgh

*a Wee Guide to Macbeth and Early Scotland*

© Martin Coventry 1999
Published by **GOBLINSHEAD**
130B Inveresk Road
Musselburgh EH21 7AY
Scotland
*tel* 0131 665 2894; *fax* 0131 653 6566; *email* goblinshead@sol.co.uk

British Library Cataloguing in Publication Data
A catalogue record for this book is available from the British Library.

ISBN 1 899874 22 4

Typeset by **GOBLINSHEAD** using Desktop Publishing

## WEE GUIDES
**William Wallace**
**The Picts**
**Scottish History**
**The Jacobites**
**Robert Burns**
**Mary, Queen of Scots**
**Robert the Bruce**
**Haunted Castles of Scotland**
**Old Churches and Abbeys of Scotland**
**Castles and Mansions of Scotland**
*New for 1999*
**Prehistoric Scotland**
**Macbeth and Early Scotland**
**Whisky**
*Also published*
**The Castles of Scotland 2E (£14.50)**
**Haunted Places of Scotland (£7.50)**
**The Hebrides (£5.95)**
**William Wallace – Champion of Scotland (£6.95)**

*a Wee Guide to*
# Macbeth and Early Scotland

# Contents

List of Illustrations     i
Acknowledgements     ii
How to Use the Book     iii
Preface     iv

Calendar of Events     2
Chapter 1 – Macbeth's Scotland     5
Chapter 2 – The Peoples of Scotland     10
Chapter 3 – Saints and Holy Men     17
Chapter 4 – Sinners and Warlords     22
Chapter 5 – Vikings, Scots, Picts     29
Chapter 6 – Kin Strife and Wars     34
Chapter 7 – Duncan, Macbeth and Malcolm Canmore     39

Places of Interest     43

Index     85

# List of Illustrations

Macbeth (Martin, NGS)
*Front Cover*
Macbeth (Hall, SNPG)
*Frontispiece*

Processional Frieze, Sir William
  Hole (SNPG)    *Before page 1*
**Map 1 – Early Scotland**    **4**
Macbeth (Martin, NGS)    5
Macbeth (Hall, SNPG)    6
Glamis Castle    8
Malcolm Canmore, engraving by
  Miller (SNPG)    9
Broch of Mousa (Reed)    11
Hadrian's Wall (Miller)    12
Entrance, Dunadd    15
**Map 2 – Early Scotland**    **16**
Whithorn    17
St Columba preaching to the Picts,
  Sir William Hole (SNPG)    19
Statue of St Cuthbert, Lindisfarne
  (Miller)    21
Processional Frieze, Sir William
  Hole (SNPG)    22
Processional Frieze, Sir William
  Hole (SNPG)    23
Boar Carving, Dunadd    25
Hexham Abbey    26
**Map 3 – Early Scotland**    **28**
Iona Abbey    29
**Map 4 – England**    **30**
Dunnottar Castle    33
Bamburgh Castle    34

Edinburgh Castle    36
Duncan I, engraving by Taylor
  (SNPG)    38
Landing of St Margaret at
  Queensferry, Sir William Hole
  (SNPG)    41
Processional Frieze, Sir William
  Hole (SNPG)    42
**Map 5 – Places of Interest**    **44**
Applecross    47
Brechin Cathedral    49
Cawdor Castle    51
Dunadd (Reed)    54
Dunblane Cathedral    55
Dunfermline Abbey    56
Dunnottar Castle    58
Dunstaffnage Castle    59
Elgin Cathedral    62
Glasgow Cathedral    64
Holy Island    66
Beach, Iona    68
Keills Chapel    69
Kildalton Cross    70
Monymusk Church    72
Arch, St Blane's, Bute    76
St Vigeans Church    77
Maiden Stone    80
Alnwick Castle    84

# Acknowledgements

Many thanks to Martin Coventry and Joyce Miller at Goblinshead.

*Illustrations reproduced by kind permission of:*
The National Gallery of Scotland for *Macbeth* by John Martin (front cover and page 5). The Scottish National Portrait Gallery for *Macbeth* by Hall (frontispiece and page 6); *Malcolm Canmore* by Miller (page 9) and *Duncan I* by Taylor (page 38). Also Scottish National Portrait Gallery for *Processional Frieze* (pages before page 1, 22, 23, 42), *The Landing of St Margaret at Queensferry* (page 41) and *St Columba Preaching to the Picts* (page 19) by Sir William Hole.

Photographs of Broch of Mousa and Dunadd by Dave Reed (pages 11 and 54); Hadrian's Wall and St Cuthbert, Lindisfarne by Joyce Miller (pages 12 and 21). Other photographs by Martin Coventry. Maps and design by Martin Coventry.

# How to Use the Book

*The book is divided into two sections:*

- The text (pages 1-41) describes the background and principal events and people associated with the earliest kingdoms in Scotland. It covers the earliest peoples; the coming of Christianity; feuds and battles between the various peoples; Viking invasions; later wars and the succession of kings and finally the reigns of Duncan, Macbeth and Malcolm Canmore. Four maps (pages 4, 16, 28 & 30) locate the most important places mentioned in the text. A calendar of events summarises the period chronologically (pages 2-3).

- Places to visit in Scotland associated with Macbeth and early Scotland (pages 43-80) lists over 70 sites. There is a map (page 44) which illustrates their location. Information includes access, opening, facilities and a brief description. Other sites in Scotland are listed (pages 81-84) and there is also a list of English sites (page 84). Admission charges are as follows: £ = £3.50 or under; ££ = £3.50-£5.00; £££ = more than £5.00

An index (pages 85-86) lists all the main people, places and events.

## Warning

While the information in this book was believed to be correct at time of going to press – and was checked, where possible, with the visitor attractions – opening times and facilities, or other information, may differ from that included. All information should be checked with the visitor attractions before embarking on any journey. Inclusion in the text is no indication whatsoever that a site is open to the public or that it should be visited. Some sites are in difficult and inaccessible locations, while ruinous buildings can be in a dangerous condition. Care should be taken when visiting any site. Inclusion or exclusion of any site should not be considered as a comment or judgement on that site. Locations on the maps are approximate.

# Preface

This wee book is about Macbeth and early Scotland, from the Romans until the death of Malcolm Canmore at the end of the 11th century. Macbeth, himself, is the best known of the characters from this time, yet this is due only to Shakespeare's famous play. Most of the events surrounding him were invented, either by earlier chroniclers such as Boece or by the bard himself. Macbeth was no better or worse than his contemporaries, and ruled for some seventeen years – a long reign for the times. If truth be told, very little is known about the real Macbeth.

Macbeth, himself, was from a long line of kings, stretching back to Fergus MacErc, king of Dalriada, in the early 6th century. Sources for this time are unreliable and conflicting, consisting of sagas, king lists and chronicles, some of them compiled hundreds of years after the events. The number of kings, saints and princes is large and complex – often they had the same name. I have tried to keep the narrative as simple as possible, while still covering all the main events.

The story of early Scotland from the mists of the Iron Age to the birth of the medieval kingdom of Scots is a fascinating one. This was an age of high adventure: of warfare, feuding and raiding: few kings died of old age in the days of Macbeth.

*CS, Musselburgh, May 1999.*

'Will all great Neptune's ocean wash this blood
Clean from my hand? No, this my hand will rather
The multitudinous seas incarnadine,
Making the green one red.'

# a *Wee Guide* to
# *Macbeth and*
# *Early Scotland*

# Calendar of Events

| | |
|---|---|
| 55 BC | Julius Caesar invades south of Britain |
| 79 AD | Agricola invades Caledonia |
| 84 AD | Roman victory against Caledonian tribes at Mon Graupius |
| 122-136 AD | Building of Hadrian's Wall |
| 140 AD | Building of Antonine Wall |
| 300 AD | First mention of Picts |
| 360 AD | First mention of Scots |
| 367-407 AD | Roman legions withdrawn; Picts and Scots overrun Roman province of Britain |
| 400-430 AD | Hadrian's Wall finally abandoned; St Ninian active in Galloway; Scots first settled in Dalriada |
| 503 | Dalriada established in Scotland; death of Fergus, son of Erc, king of Dalriada |
| 550 | Angles settle in Northumberland |
| 561 | Battle of Cul Drebene – Columba involved |
| 563 | Columba established at Iona; Columba believed to have converted northern Picts |
| 570-600 | St Mungo active among Britons |
| 574 | Columba ordains Aeden, son of Gabhrain, at Dunadd as king of Dalriada |
| 597 | Columba dies |
| 600 | Northern Britons, led by the Gododdin, slaughtered at Catterick |
| 603 | Battle of Degastan: Aeden defeated by Ethelfrith, king of Northumbria |
| 634-651 | St Aidan active among Northumbrians |
| 637 | Scots of Dalriada lose control of their Irish lands |
| 638 | Northumbrians control Lothian |
| 642 | Battle of Strathcarron: Donald Breac, king of Dalriada, slaughtered by Britons |
| 663 | Synod of Whitby: Roman practices of church asserted over Celtic belief |
| 672 | Picts massacred by Ecgfrith of Northumbria |
| 685 | Battle of Nechtansmere: Picts under Brude, son of Bile, defeat Ecgfrith and the Northumbrians |

| | |
|---|---|
| 711 | Picts slaughtered at battle on the plains of Manaw by the Northumbrians |
| 793- | Raids by Vikings begin: Lindisfarne and Iona sacked |
| 811-820 | Dunkeld founded as major ecclesiastical centre; Constantine, son of Fergus, king of Dalriada and Picts |
| 820-834 | St Andrews becomes important ecclesiastical centre; Angus, son of Fergus, king of Dalriada and Picts |
| 843 | Union of Picts and Scots: Kenneth king of both peoples |
| 914-918 | Battles of Corbridge: fights between Scots, Northumbrians and Vikings |
| 920 | Constantine enters treaty with Edward the Elder of England: Scots subject to England? |
| 934 | Athelstan, king of Wessex, invades Scotland |
| 937 | Battle of Brunanburgh: Scots, Britons and Vikings defeated by Athelstan |
| 945 | Edmund of England invades Cumbria and grants it to Scots |
| 954-962 | Scots occupy Lothian |
| 971 | Constantine II of Scots plunders England |
| 973 | Kenneth II enters treaty with English king Edgar |
| 985-989 | Viking raids continue |
| 1018 | Battle of Carham: Malcolm II of Scots defeats English and takes Lothian; Scots acquire Strathclyde |
| 1034 | Duncan becomes king of Scots |
| 1040 | Duncan defeated and killed by Macbeth at Spynie; Macbeth king of Scots |
| 1054 | Macbeth defeated at Dunsinane? by Malcolm Canmore and English force |
| 1057 | Macbeth slain at Lumphanan |
| 1057-8 | Lulach king of Scots but slain in 1058; Malcolm III becomes king of Scots |
| 1066 | Battle of Hastings: English under Harold defeated by Normans led by William the Conqueror |
| 1068 | Malcolm marries Margaret, sister of Saxon heir to English throne: Malcolm invades England 1061-1069 |
| 1072 | Malcolm Canmore becomes subject to William the Conqueror after invasion from England |
| 1093 | Malcolm Canmore slain at Alnwick; death of Queen Margaret |

# *Map 1: Early Scotland (chapters 1-2)*

SHETLAND

Lerwick

ORKNEY

Kirkwall

PENTLAND FIRTH

Thurso
*Caithness*

*Sutherland*
Wick

LEWIS

Stornoway

HARRIS

NORTH UIST

Ullapool

*Ross*

Tain
Burghead
Fraserburgh

Rosemarkie
Forres
Elgin
*Banff*
*Buchan*

RAASAY
Cawdor

SOUTH UIST

SKYE

Inverness
M o r a y
? Mons Graupius

*Aberdeenshire*
Aberdeen

HEBRIDES

BARRA

Urquhart

Lumphanan

Dunnottar

*Mearns*

*Great Glen*

*Atholl*

*P i c t l a n d*
Brechin

LISMORE

HIGHLANDS
Aberlemno
Montrose

Dunkeld
Meigle
Glamis

MULL

Dunstaffnage
Dunsinane
*Angus*
Arbroath

IONA

Dunollie
Scone
Dundee

*Dalriada*
Perth
St Andrews

COLONSAY

*Argyll*
Forteviot
Abernethy
Cupar

*Strathearn*
*Fife*

Dunadd
Dunblane

JURA

Stirling
Dunfermline

Dumbarton
FORTH

ISLAY

Tarbert
Dunimarle
Edinburgh
Traprain
Dunbar

BUTE
Glasgow
*Lothian*

ARRAN
Lanark
Melrose
Berwick

CLYDE

Ayr

*S t r a t h c l y d e*

Dunaverty

*Northumberland*

**ENGLAND**

*Galloway*
Hadrian's Wall
Hadrian's Wall

Stranraer

Whithorn
SOLWAY
Carlisle

*Cumbria*

# 1 – *Macbeth's Scotland*

*'By the pricking of my thumbs,
Something wicked this way comes.'*

Macbeth – along possibly with Kenneth MacAlpin and St Columba – is one of the few well-known characters from early Scotland. Yet Macbeth is (probably) a much maligned figure, most of the information about him coming from Shakespeare's famous play (which you must not mention!). The play was written for James VI at the beginning of the 17th century, just after James had united Scotland and England under one king. Shakespeare himself is not responsible for these inaccuracies, or at least embellishments. Chroniclers such as John of Fordoun (died 1387), Walter Bower (15th century), and particularly Hector Boece

*Macbeth and Banquo*

(who died in 1536) tried to establish an unbroken line of kings all the way back to Fergus MacErc in the 6th century – and beyond, even, to a mythological past and to Pharaoh's daughter Scotia. This was particularly important to give legitimacy both to the kings of Scots and to the Stewarts. James VI's line went through Duncan and Malcolm Canmore, rather than Macbeth. The English chronicler Holinshed copied these passages from Boece, and Shakespeare used Holinshed's text as his inspiration. Consequently, Macbeth was seen as a usurper and villain, as the later kings were not related directly to him, and his name was blackened beyond recognition.

In fact, for the times, Macbeth (Macbeth means 'son of life') seems to have been an able king, and ruled for some seventeen years or so. This reign may not seem very long in more settled and peaceful ages. There were, however, fifteen kings of Scots from 843 until 1040. Bearing in mind that one king, Constantine II, ruled for 43 years, this means that the average length of rule was just over ten years. Nor did many of these kings die peacefully:

*Macbeth – engraving*

virtually all were slain in battle or murdered by their rivals. What is true is that Duncan was neither old nor was he murdered in his bed: Duncan was mortally wounded in battle against Macbeth, and probably died from his wounds at or near Elgin.

Duncan had not ruled well, nor was he in anyway a paragon of virtue: no snowy bearded, wise old king. Indeed Malcolm II had murdered Duncan's rivals in an attempt to secure Duncan, his grandson, as undisputed ruler. Duncan made war on Thorfinn the Mighty – Thorfinn Ravenfeeder – who was earl of Orkney and controlled a large island kingdom, which stretched from the northern isles down through the Hebrides. Duncan was defeated in a battle near Burghead in Moray by Thorfinn, and then by Macbeth, who may have been Thorfinn's half-brother. Macbeth was then proclaimed king. Duncan's son, Malcolm, fled to Northumberland in England, which was ruled by King Cnut or Canute. Incidentally, King Canute was a Christian ruler and his efforts to turn back the tide were actually to show how powerless all mortals were compared to the forces of nature – so showing the omnipotence of God as he had created nature.

The dynastic conflicts stemmed, at least partly, from the tradition of succession among the kings of Scots. Primogeniture had not been established as the means of descent, and any able man from the royal house could be king. To make succession clearer – and less bloody – the existing king chose his successor, his 'tanaise'. This, however, left anyone with a blood claim to the throne, either through father or mother, as a potential rival. Both Macbeth and Gruoch, his wife, had a good claim to the throne – and anyway the most important attribute to maintaining the throne was prowess in battle. Gruoch was the granddaughter of Kenneth III, who had been slain, along with his son Giric, by Malcolm II. Macbeth, too, had royal blood, and it is likely that he was a son of Donada, daughter of Malcolm himself (hence he was half-brother to Thorfinn, who was her son by Sigurd the Stout). Duncan may have chosen to attack Macbeth, his cousin and possible rival, but was himself worsted and slain.

There is no evidence that Lady Macbeth – Gruoch – was the scheming, manipulative woman portrayed by Shakespeare – certainly no evidence she ended her life desolate and insane: this appears to be entirely an invention of Hector Boece, a chronicler in the 16th century. If anything Scotland prospered under Macbeth: he is said to have strengthened the rule of law and to have made a pilgrimage to Rome. Crinan, father of Duncan, made trouble for Macbeth, but Crinan's rising was easily put down and he was himself killed.

It is highly unlikely that two of Macbeth's most evil acts (at least in the play) – the murder of Lady MacDuff and her children, and the slaying of Banquo – ever took place. The site of the murder of Lady

*Glamis*

MacDuff, incidentally, has been given as at Dunimarle or at Cupar, which are both in Fife, but there is no early record that this event ever took place. Similarly there is no historical evidence to support even the existence of Banquo or Fleance (Banquo's son), or how the later kings were supposedly descended from them. Again Boece was attempting to give the Stewart kings a greater legitimacy than simply marrying a daughter of Robert the Bruce. It also seems unlikely that Macbeth had any association with either Cawdor or Glamis. Cawdor Castle was not built until some centuries after Macbeth's death, and although the present Glamis Castle probably stands on the site of a much older stronghold, there is similarly little evidence to support any visit, never mind being the scene of Duncan's murder.

The future Malcolm III – Malcolm Canmore – did not have enough support in Scotland to get rid of Macbeth, and he turned to the English king for help and was supported by Siward of Northumberland. Initially this alliance was not successful and Siward, invading in support of Malcolm, was defeated by Macbeth and his own son slain. This did, however, weaken Macbeth considerably. Malcolm, himself, brought Macbeth to battle in 1054 or later, possibly near Dunsinane, and Macbeth was defeated – but not killed. What then appears to have happened is that Macbeth ruled the north, and Malcolm the south. Three years later, in 1057, Macbeth was finally defeated and killed at

Lumphanan, and Malcolm ruled the kingdom of Scots. Fortunately for Malcolm, Thorfinn the Mighty was already dead or things might have then gone very differently.

Macbeth and Gruoch apparently did have children, but their claim passed to Lulach the Fool, Gruoch's son by her first marriage. Lulach was slain in 1058. Malcolm was now

*Malcolm Canmore*

undisputed king and Scotland had more or less reached its southern border. The Hebrides and Orkney and Shetland, however, were to remain in the possession of the Norse kings for several more centuries.

Macbeth's Scotland had been forged by hundreds of years of fighting, kin strife and raiding, the melding of the kingdoms and lands of Picts, Scots, Britons and Angles. Petty kings and lordlings rose and fell, the great ecclesiastical centre of Iona flowered then withered in Viking raids, the powerful kingdom of the Picts flourished for centuries but has left little trace in these later years. The Picts themselves are a mystery, and are believed by some to be the remnants of an indigenous people out of prehistory. To understand Macbeth's Scotland, it is necessary to return to events a thousand years and more before.

# 2 – The Peoples of Scotland

The first inhabitants of the lands now known as Scotland arrived in the Middle Stone Age (Mesolithic) period, some 7000 or so years ago. Evidence for their visits – it is assumed they were nomads who lived in caves or rough shelters – is restricted to tools, weapons and middens. Some 1000 years later in the New Stone Age (Neolithic), they began to settle in Scotland: farmers who brought domestic animals and grew crops; although hunting and fishing were also vitally important. The prehistoric village at Skara Brae on Orkney is a monument to their skill and ingenuity: their dwellings, built of fine drystone masonry, have central hearths and stone dressers, 'beds' and boxes, and a drainage system.

These early people also built elaborate chambered cairns for burying their dead. These take many forms and were adapted through the centuries as methods of 'disposing' of the dead changed in the Bronze Age. Particularly fine examples include Maes Howe and Quoyness in Orkney, Nether Largie in Argyll, Barpa Langass on North Uist, and Clava Cairns near Inverness. Stone circles and single stones were also erected, some associated with burials, others as memorials, others apparently as astronomical observatories. Callanish, on Lewis, is the finest complex of stones in Scotland, but there are other impressive circles at Brodgar and Stenness on Orkney Mainland and at Machrie Moor on Arran.

About 1000 BC the climate appears to have deteriorated and there was increased pressure on good land. There may have been an influx of peoples from the continent. Whatever the reason, people began to live in hill forts and other fortified sites. The inhabitants of Scotland also started to use iron for their weapons and tools. The centuries passed, and fortified sites were developed and brochs and duns constructed from about 100 BC. Brochs are round drystone defensive towers, the best surviving example is at Mousa on Shetland, although there also fine brochs at Dun Carloway on Lewis, at Glenelg in Lochaber, and on Orkney and Shetland. Duns are small forts or fortified homesteads, with a wall defending an enclosure or cutting off a promontory. These settlements were occupied for centuries, sometimes into medieval and

*Broch of Mousa, Shetland*

even early modern times. It is not clear why brochs were built or who they were to defend against – it has been suggested it may have been Roman slave ships. These societies were organised around a chief or king who would have had a following of warriors. As well as farming and trade, they also raided their neighbours' settlements, carrying off booty and taking cattle and slaves.

The Romans invaded the south of Britain in 55 BC under Julius Caesar, then moved north. By 79 AD Julius Agricola, Roman Governor of Britain, advanced into the area which we now know as Scotland and attempted to crush any opposition. The Romans had conquered the Britons of the south, and formed what became a wealthy Roman province. They encountered a group of fierce and warlike tribes in the north of Briton and called them Caledonians. The Romans did not have it all their own way: it is widely believed the Ninth Roman Legion was slaughtered in Galloway in 83 AD.

The Romans returned and a year later – according to their own account – routed the Caledonian army at the battle of Mons Graupius, killing 10,000 of the enemy with a loss of only some 340 men. Calgacus was the leader of the Caledonians – if the Roman chronicler Tacitus is to be believed – and is the first named 'Scot'. Despite this crushing victory (the scale of which Tacitus most likely exaggerated), the

Romans were still harried and hard-pressed by the local tribes. The Romans built forts at Inveresk, east of Edinburgh, Inchtuthill, north-east of Perth, as well as at Newstead, near Melrose, to consolidate their gains, although in 105 AD the fort at Newstead was burnt.

The Emperor Hadrian found the Caledonian tribes so troublesome that he had a wall built – Hadrian's Wall –

*Hadrian's Wall*

across the north of England, from Newcastle in the east to the Solway Firth in the west, with forts and mile castles. This wall, however, never formed the border between the medieval kingdoms or modern countries of Scotland and England.

The Romans invaded the north again in 139 AD and tried to capture the lands between Hadrian's Wall and the Rivers Forth and Clyde. They built another wall, the Antonine Wall, but this was eventually overrun by the Caledonian tribes. The forts along this wall were occupied in 154-5 AD, and possibly again in 185-207 AD.

By 368 AD the Roman hold on Britain was loosening with troubles at home and the withdrawal of Roman forces. Hadrian's Wall was finally abandoned about 400 AD. The Picts, Scots and Saxons attacked the south, ravaged the lands of the Roman province and plundered London of its riches. Little of Roman culture, learning or influence had ever penetrated into Scotland beyond the Forth and Clyde – and the little that had was soon lost.

The Picts were first mentioned by the Romans about 300 AD as the people or tribes who held the north. It is not clear whether the Picts were a united people or a loose confederation of tribes who banded together to defend themselves against the Romans. Indeed, very little is known about the Picts altogether, but it appears they were one of the groups of ancient people now known as Celtic, of whom the Britons (Bretons, Welsh, Cumbrians, Cornish and Strathclydian) and the Scots (as well as Irish Gaelic, Manx, and perhaps the Basques) were also related. They spoke a language akin to Welsh (Brythonic Gaelic), although some accounts, and historians, also give them an ancient, pre-Indo-European tongue, although evidence for this is disputed. The concentration of place names with the element 'Aber', 'Pit' or other Brythonic elements are concentrated thickly in the north-east of Scotland, Angus and Fife – which was the heart of their kingdom.

The name *Picti* or 'painted men', as the Romans called them, may have been a general term of abuse for any folk beyond the ken of their empire. Tattooing and body decoration were a feature of many cultures, but were not what was acceptable within the Roman Empire. By the 3rd century the Picts were divided into the Caledonians of the north and the Maeatae of the south.

The Irish called the Picts the *Cruithni* – the 'people of designs' – but it is not known what they called themselves. The Picts had major strongholds or centres at Inverness, Burghead, Urquhart, Dunkeld, Scone, Dunfermline, Forteviot and Abernethy. They are believed to have used matrilineal descent of inheritance for their kings, where the line descended through the mother.

Various reasons have been given for this system of succession, one being that they were a promiscuous lot and that while paternity of any child is never certain there is never any doubt about the mother. Another suggestion is that the Picts came from Scythia, near the Black Sea, and migrated through Europe before coming to Ireland. Here they helped the Irish against their enemies in what is now Scotland. In reward the Irish king gave them lands in Scotland. The Picts were given the widows of slain Irish warriors as their wives. This was all on the condition that they chose their kings from the female (or Irish) line. It seems likely that this story was to try to prove some superiority of the kings of Scots (Dalriada) over the Picts – and it all seems highly unlikely. Besides which, the evidence for matrilineal descent is not great.

At its height their kingdom (or those lands they controlled) of Pictland stretched from Shetland and Orkney down to the Forth and Clyde, and perhaps through Galloway as well. Skye and the Outer Hebrides were also occupied although the Picts' power may have never been consolidated here. The Hebrides and Orkney and Shetland do not appear to have been part of their ancient kingdom. The Picts do not seem to have settled in the southern isles of the Inner Hebrides, Strathclyde and Lothian, although the Pentland Hills, to the south of Edinburgh, (and also the Pentland Firth) may derive from their name. The legendary king Cruithne ruled over the lands, and the Pictish kingdom was traditionally divided into seven ancient provinces on his death: the area that each of his seven sons controlled. Fib ruled over Fife; Cat Caithness; and Fortriu the lands round the Forth. His other sons were Fotlaig who controlled Atholl and Strathearn; Fiddach Moray; Ce Aberdeenshire and Banff and Buchan; and Circenn Angus.

The enduring legacy of the Picts – most material remains of their settlements are little different from their British or later Scottish contemporaries – is their magnificent and enigmatic symbol stones. The sculpted stones at Aberlemno and elsewhere are fine examples of the mason's art. There are excellent museums at St Vigeans, near Arbroath; Meigle; and Groam House, at Rosemarkie, which house collections of their stones, as well as in the Museum of Scotland. On Skye and the Outer Hebrides there are Pictish remains including sculptured stones, such as Clach Ard on Skye as well as a carved stone on Raasay.

The Britons were also an ancient Celtic people, giving their name to Britain, and in Scotland they held Strathclyde and Lothian. Their northern kingdom was known either as Strathclyde or as Cumbria or indeed both – it is not always clear whether Cumbria covered only the lands south of the Solway or included Strathclyde as well. The Britons of Strathclyde spoke a language akin to Welsh, and were said to have been descended from the Novantae of south-west Scotland, who occupied the area in Roman times. Lothian was controlled from

Traprain Law in East Lothian by the British people known as the Gododdin or Votadini.

At one time British kingdoms stretched from Cornwall, in the far south of Britain, all the way to Dumbarton and Edinburgh in Scotland. The main fortresses of Strathclyde were at Dumbarton and at Carlisle, which is now over the border in northern England.

After the Legions left, the Britons of the disintegrating former Roman province were harried and attacked by incomers from the Continent: the Angles, Saxons and Jutes, who settled along the east coast forcing the Britons to the west.

The Scots from Ireland (which, like the north part of Scotland, was never held by the Romans) are mentioned about 360 AD by the Romans – although again it was not a name they then used of themselves: it is said to mean 'pirates'. The Celtic Scots, who spoke a different branch of Gaelic (Goidelic, a group of languages along with Irish Gaelic and Manx), raided the coasts of Britain (and most likely Pictland)

*Entrance, Dunadd*

from about 300 AD, and probably began to establish themselves in the southern Hebrides and Argyll from this time by pushing out the Britons. By 400 AD these Scots had settled in this area, and their kingdom was known as Dalriada, from the *Dal Riata* tribe of Antrim in the north of Ireland. They had strongholds at Dunadd, Dunollie, Dunstaffnage, Dunaverty and Tarbert, which were all to be besieged and burnt at different times. Dunadd is an interesting hill fort, while the other sites were reused for medieval strongholds.

These kingdoms, peoples and tribes, would spend much of their time – and vigour – fighting each other down the following centuries.

# Map 2: Early Scotland (chapters 3-4)

SHETLAND

Lerwick

ORKNEY

Kirkwall

PENTLAND FIRTH

Thurso

*Caithness*

*Sutherland*

Wick

LEWIS

Stornoway

HARRIS

NORTH UIST

Ullapool

*Ross*

Tain

Burghead

Fraserburgh

Rosemarkie

Forres

Elgin

*Banff*

Deer

SOUTH UIST

RAASAY

Applecross

Inverness

*Moray*

Mortlach

*Aberdeenshire*

SKYE

HEBRIDES

Urquhart

Aberdeen

BARRA

*Great Glen*

Dunnottar

*Mearns*

*Atholl*

*Pictland*

Brechin

HIGHLANDS

Nechtansmere

Montrose

LISMORE

Dunstaffnage

Dunkeld

Glendochart

*Angus*

Arbroath

IONA

Dunollie

**Dalriada**

Scone

Dundee

Garvellachs

*Argyll*

Perth

Forteviot

*Fife*

St Andrews

COLONSAY

Dunadd

*Strathearn*

Abernethy

Dundurn

Dunblane

*Manaw*

Dunfermline

JURA

Eilean Mor

Tarbert

Dumbarton

Culross

FORTH

Dunbar

ISLAY

*Lothian*

Glasgow

Abercorn

Edinburgh

BUTE

Lanark

Melrose

Berwick

ARRAN

CLYDE

Ayr

*Strathclyde*

*Kyle*

Degastan?

Dunaverty

*Northumberland*

**ENGLAND**

**Galloway**

Ruthwell

Stranraer

SOLWAY

Carlisle

Kirkmadrine

Whithorn

*Cumbria*

# 3 - Saints and Holy Men

Christianity had probably arrived in the north of Britain through the Roman garrisons and settlements along Hadrian's Wall and into southern Scotland and Galloway. The northern lands, however, were mostly or even entirely pagan. The Romans called them druids and despised them for their barbaric beliefs, which included human sacrifice – it was much more civilised to feed Christians to lions. St Barr, on converting the folk of Barra, is said to have dissuaded them from cannibalism. From the 5th century, or possibly earlier, Christianity found popularity in Scotland. The most famous of these early missionaries in Scotland was St Ninian, but St Patrick is probably better known throughout Britain and, of course, Ireland.

By 430 AD, St Ninian, a Briton, had been active in Galloway, converting the Britons (as well as possibly the southern Picts) to Christianity. Ninian had been educated in Rome, and founded a religious house at Whithorn, *Candida Casa* – 'white house'. It was called 'Candida Casa' because the walls of his church were whitewashed. Ninian was bishop at Whithorn, but died in 432 AD. Whithorn remained an important

*Whithorn*

religious centre, and was a place of pilgrimage in medieval times: there are the ruins of a fine medieval church. It is also here and at Kirkmadrine, south of Stranraer, that the earliest Christian stones in Scotland are found. St Ninian's Cave, south-west of Whithorn, is traditionally associated with the saint.

In the same year, St Patrick, who is believed to have been born at Kilpatrick, east of Dumbarton, converted many of the Irish to Christianity. Earlier St Patrick had criticised the then Christian king of Strathclyde, Ceretic, for crimes such as selling Christian slaves to the Scots and the Picts.

In 503 many Scots left Ireland and settled in Argyll, joining with others who had emigrated before them. Their new kingdom was known as Dalriada, and their king, Fergus, son of Erc, reputedly brought with him the Stone of Destiny. Many of the Scots were already Christian as St Patrick had been active in Ireland from 430.

St Brendan, who died in 577, was another priest from Ireland, who journeyed to the western and northern isles. He is commemorated in place names such as Kilbrandon Sound, east of Arran, and Kilbrennan, on Mull. St Brendan founded a monastic community on one of the Garvellach Isles: Columba's mother, Eithne, is believed to be buried there.

The Britons were beset by an invasion of Angles, who held much of the east of England by 547, having established footholds there for some twenty years. Ida became the ruler of the English kingdom of Bernicia or Northumberland, which included lands from the Firth of Forth to the River Tees in the north of England. His capital was at the fine defensive rocky crag of Bamburgh – the site of which is now occupied by a massive medieval castle. The Angles were still pagans.

St Columba, who was related to Fergus, son of Erc, through his grandmother, was born at Donegal in 521 and was therefore of royal birth. He founded monasteries in Ireland before an argument with King Diarmid, after his implication in the bloody battle of Cul Drebene, led to him leaving Ireland. He settled on Iona, determined that he should go where he could not see Ireland: he is said to have briefly stopped at Colonsay on his way north, but he could still make out the hills of his

*St Columba Preaching to the Picts*

home. Columba brought with him the Celtic form of the Christian church which had flourished in Ireland, which involved the setting up of monasteries, usually on remote and isolated islands or locations.

According to his biographer Adamnan, Columba converted the northern Picts, ruled by King Brude, son of Maelchon. His stronghold was believed to have been at what is now Urquhart Castle or possibly at the hill fort at Craig Phaidraig, which is near Inverness. Columba is said to have confronted a kelpie or serpent in Loch Ness, the first mention of a monster there, and to have defeated Bride's wizard, Briochan, in a magical duel. St Drostan was Columba's nephew and active among the Picts: he founded a monastic establishment at Deer – later the site of a medieval abbey. The Book of Deer is an 11th- or 12th-century manuscript of St John's gospel and parts of other gospels – it is held in Cambridge University Library.

St Columba ordained Aedan, son of Gabhrain, the sixth king of the Dalriadian Scots, at Dunadd. Still surviving at the fortress are a footprint and bowl carved in living rock which are said to have been associated with the inauguration ceremony. The Stone of Destiny is also believed to have been used in the ritual. There is also the faint trace of a rock-cut boar (which, incidentally, appears to be Pictish in its execution).

Iona became the centre of Christianity in Scotland, and annals written here from 575 are the basis of the Book of Kells, an illuminated manuscript now in Trinity College, Dublin. Columba died in 597, and Adamnan, a contemporary, wrote Columba's biography, which provides a record of this period. The present restored abbey of Iona dates from medieval times, but many Scots, Irish and Norse kings are buried here, including both Duncan and Macbeth.

Columba was not alone in trying to convert the north to Christianity. St Moluag, who died in 592, came from Ireland and established a monastic community on the Argyll island of Lismore, which he named 'great garden'. He is also associated with Rosemarkie and Mortlach. His pastoral staff was long preserved on Lismore. Moluag is said to have been a rival of Columba, and only managed to reach the island first by cutting off his finger and hurling it on to the island. The later Cathedral of the Isles was dedicated to the saint, and the choir, much reduced in height, is still used as the parish church.

St Rule, said to have been a disciple of Columba, established a church in the 6th century at Kinrymont – St Andrews – bringing with him the relics of St Andrew. An alternative version is that the relics were brought north in the 8th century by Acca, bishop of Hexham.

St Mungo (which means 'dear friend'), also known as Kentigern, was the son of St Enoch or Theneu, a daughter of a king of Lothian, who fell pregnant although unwed. Mungo was brought up and taught at Culross by St Serf, and was active in attempting to convert the Britons of Strathclyde, Cumbria and Wales. Glasgow Cathedral is dedicated to him, and is said to have been founded by the saint in 573. The present splendid cathedral is mainly medieval, but is built over Mungo's tomb

St Cormac was also active in the Hebrides, and is associated with Eilean Mor, off the coast of Knapdale, where he is said to be buried. St Blane, another contemporary, had a monastery at Kingarth on Bute.

In the 7th century St Molaise founded a monastery on the Holy Island off Arran. He was born in Dalriada and educated in Ireland, where he returned and was made abbot of a monastery. In the second half of the 7th century St Maelrubha founded a monastic settlement at Applecross, Wester Ross, and is said to have been buried there. He was also active on Skye.

St Aidan, a missionary from Iona, converted the pagan Angles of Bernicia to Christianity, and was a bishop of the Northumbrian Church from 634 until his death in 651. His work was continued by St Cuthbert, who entered a monastery at Melrose in 651. Cuthbert was made bishop of Hexham in 684, then Lindisfarne in 685. Lindisfarne, in Northumberland, became a great religious centre, and the ruins of a later priory are in the care of English Heritage and open to the public. Cuthbert was patron of Durham, and his relics are kept in the grand and impressive cathedral there.

*Statue of St Cuthbert, Lindisfarne*

# 4 – Sinners and Warlords

The kingdoms of the north were attacked from the south and east by the Angles of Northumberland. Rhiderch Hen was king of the British kingdom of Strathclyde, while in 574 Aedan, son of Gabhrain (Gabhrain was himself killed by the Picts), was king of Dalriada. By 585 Brude, son Maelchon, the king of Picts, who had been converted by Columba, was dead. The British kingdom of Rheged, which stretched from Catterick to Galloway, fell to Northumbrian invaders in 590 and its ruler Urien was slain at Lindisfarne.

The Britons felt threatened by the seemingly unstoppable advance of the kingdom of Northumberland. In 600, the northern Britons from Strathclyde and Cumbria, led by the Gododdin of Lothian, marched south but were heavily defeated at Catterick. In 603, Aedan, son of Gabhrain, king of Dalriada, also raised an army and went south to halt the expansion of power of the Northumbrians. Aedan had fought for many years against the Picts although he married a Pictish princess, marking the way forward for the coming together of the two peoples. Aedan was supported by the Britons of Strathclyde, but he was utterly defeated by Ethelfrith at Degastan with the loss of two of his sons. This

*Mural of characters from Scottish history (William Hole)*

defeat led to the beginning of a sustained Northumbrian expansion northwards, and by 606 Aedan, king of Dalriada, was dead.

Warfare and strife, however, were not confined to invading and raiding: it also involved kin strife and internal feuding. Ethelfrith was slain by his rival Edwin, and Edwin's rivals, including Eanfrith, Oswald and Oswiu, sought refuge in exile among the Scots and Picts. Oswald became king of Northumbria in 634.

Donald Breac became king of Dalriada in 634, but Donald's reign was a disaster for his realm. In 637 Dalriada lost control of its Irish homeland, and the Scots were defeated by the Picts in 635 and 638. In 638 the kingdom of Northumbria pushed its border northwards, besieged the fortress of Edinburgh and took the province or kingdom of Lothian.

In 641 Oswald, himself, was slain in battle against the Mercians, and was succeeded by his brother Oswiu in Bernicia – the lands of modern Northumberland and Berwickshire – then over all Northumbria from 655 until his death in 670. In 653 Tarlorgen, son of Eanfrith, was made king of Picts by Oswiu, his uncle, but Tarlorgen was not apparently a popular choice and was not to rule for long – he was dead by 657. In 658 Oswiu invaded Pictland again and subdued the greater part of that kingdom. Another of Oswiu's choices, called Drest, was forced upon the Picts in about 665.

Meanwhile Donald Breac had invaded Strathclyde in 642 and was slain by the Britons under King Owen at the battle of Strathcarron (Strathearn). The power of Dalriada was smashed and was not to be rebuilt for several decades.

The strife was not restricted to kings and lordlings, but also spread to the church. The Celtic and Roman church fought over the dating of Easter, the shape of the tonsure, baptismal rites and the ceremony for consecrating bishops – although much of its importance was also political. Oswiu of Northumbria (the lands of his kingdom included Whitby in Yorkshire), although sympathetic to the Celtic church, decided to have the matter agreed once and for all. At the Synod of Whitby in 663 the ritual and beliefs of the Roman Church were asserted over the practices of the Celtic Church. The Roman Church eventually came to dominate the whole of Scotland – although it took until the reign of David I in the 12th century. Following Whitby, Celtic monks withdrew from Northumberland and went to Iona and then to Ireland.

Oswiu died in 670, and was followed by Ecgfrith. In 672 the Picts used it as an opportunity to depose the unpopular Drest, the king who had apparently been forced on them by Oswiu. The Picts tried to reassert their independence but their army was massacred by Ecgfrith who then ravaged through Pictland. By 680 the Anglians had again seized the British kingdom of Rheged, dominated Lothian and pressed hard upon the borders of the Pictish kingdom. The Northumbrians were even confident enough to found a bishopric at Abercorn, whose bishop was Trumwin, to administer the parts of Pictland under their control. The present church here may stand on the site of the establishment. Another memorial of their church is the Ruthwell Cross, a magnificent sculpted cross at Ruthwell near Dumfries.

Pictland was sorely beset, but a king rose who would throw out the invader and establish the Picts as a powerful kingdom. Brude, son of Bile, was a son of the king of Strathclyde, and became the king of Picts and ruled until 693. One of his first acts to establish himself as undisputed ruler was a campaign to the north of Pictland, where he subdued the Orkney isles. He then turned to the west and was victorious against

*Carving of Boar, Dunadd – Pictish in its execution*

the Scots of Dalriada, who were still in disarray, even besieging and
assaulting their fortress at Dunadd in 683. The Dalriadian Scots were
brought under his sway. With his power secure, he turned his attention
to the Angles of Bernicia and Northumberland.

The Angles of Bernicia, having swept the Britons aside, tried to push
their border far to the north, but were resisted by the Picts, although
Ecgfrith had dealt ruthlessly with them in the past. Under Ecgfrith the
Northumbrians raised a large and powerful army and marched into
Pictland. The Northumbrians had previously met little effective
resistance, but they were brought to battle by Brude and the Picts in
685 at Dunnichen, also known as Nechtansmere, near the present town
of Brechin.

Brude lured the larger southern army into an area of hills and
marshes. He had a small force attack the Northumbrians, and the Picts
were quickly routed and withdrew. They were pursued by the victorious but unruly Bernicians – but it was a trick. The main part of Brude's
army, which had been hidden behind a hill, then fell upon the Anglians
and utterly defeated them: King Ecgfrith was slaughtered along with
much of his army. The carved stones at Aberlemno, which are near
Nechtansmere, probably commemorate this battle. The Picts extended
their influence south again, and continued to dominate the Scottish

kingdom of Dalriada. The Anglian bishopric at Abercorn was abandoned.

Nechtansmere should be considered, along with Hastings and Bannockburn, as one of the most important battles in Britain. It checked the expansion of Northumberland and allowed the Picts to exert their influence over the south.

Brude, son of Bile, king of Picts, died in 693, and by 706 Nechtan son of Derile was king. Brude's success did not long survive him, and in 711 the Picts were slaughtered by the Northumbrians at a battle on the plain of Manaw. In 729 Angus I, son of Fergus, became king of Picts after Nechtan, son of Derile, retired to a monastery in 724. There were five years of fighting between various factions until Angus was victorious; and he was probably the most powerful of all Pictish kings. He was an energetic ruler and crushed his enemies: in 734 he executed the ruler of Atholl by drowning him. Angus conquered Dalriada and captured Dunadd in 736 and became the first king of both Scots and Picts. So began a period of

*Hexham Abbey – it was from here that Acca brought the relics of St Andrews to Scotland.*

domination of the Scots of Dalriada by the Picts.

Acca, bishop of Hexham, is said to have brought the relics of St Andrew to Fife in 733. There was already a religious settlement here, founded by St Rule about 590: an alternative version is that St Rule brought the relics here himself. St Andrews Cathedral, once a splendid church but now a fragmentary ruin, was founded on the site of this early community. St Rule's Tower survives from an 11th-century church. There is a fine collection of early sculpture in the museum in the remains of the cloister of the the the cathedral.

The flag of Scotland, the white saltire on a blue background, represents the crucifixion of St Andrew on an 'X' shaped cross. One story is that the cross appeared in the sky before a victory by the Scots or Picts over the Norsemen, and this was attributed to the Saint's intercession.

The Northumbrian kingdom continued to expand westwards. Galloway was beset and the area of Kyle was conquered by Eadbehrt of Northumbria. In 756 Angus tried to add Strathclyde to his possessions, and he joined with the Angles and besieged Dumbarton rock. Although Dumbarton fell, his combined forces were slaughtered by the Britons a few days later and ultimately he was unsuccessful. Angus died in 761, and Aed, king of Dalriada, took this opportunity to expel the Picts and reassert the independence of Dalriada. Aed, himself, died in 777.

It was around this time that the Books of Kells was begun in Iona, then a foremost centre of learning and religion. Missionaries and saints still went about their work. St Baldred was active among the Angles of Lothian and founded a church at Tyninghame, west of Dunbar. He is also associated with the Bass Rock in the Firth of Forth. He died in 756. St Fillan, a missionary from Ireland, died in about 777. He is said to have founded a monastery at Glendochart, and his crosier is preserved in the Museum of Scotland. Christianity was now well established in all the kingdoms of the north, yet the Picts, Britons, Scots and Angles were constantly engulfed in warfare and strife.

And things were about to get worse.

# Map 3: Early Scotland (chapter 5-7)

SHETLAND

Lerwick

ORKNEY

Brough of Birsay

Kirkwall

PENTLAND FIRTH

Thurso

*Caithness*

LEWIS

Stornoway

*Sutherland*

Wick

Ullapool

HARRIS

*Ross*

Tain

NORTH UIST

RAASAY

Rosemarkie

Cullen

Fraserburgh

Forres

Elgin

*Banff*

*Buchan*

Cawdor

Dufftown

SOUTH UIST

SKYE

Inverness

*Moray*

*Aberdeenshire*

Aberdeen

HEBRIDES

Urquhart

Lumphanan

BARRA

Green Castle

Fetteresso

Fordoun

Dunnottar

*Atholl*

*Mearns*

*Pictland*

Brechin

HIGHLANDS

Glamis

Montrose

LISMORE

Dunkeld

*Angus*

Arbroath

MULL

Dunstaffnage

Luncarty

Dundee

Dunollie

Monzievaird

Scone

IONA

*Dalriada*

Fortviot

Perth

St Andrews

*Argyll*

*Strathearn*

Abernethy

*Fife*

Crail

COLONSAY

Dunadd

Dunblane

Dollar

Dunfermline

JURA

Tarbert

Dumbarton

Stirling

Dunbar

Edinburgh

ISLAY

BUTE

Glasgow

*Lothian*

ARRAN

Lanark

*Strathclyde*

Melrose

Carham

CLYDE

Ayr

Dunaverty

*Northumberland*

Brunanburgh?

**ENGLAND**

Dumfries

*Galloway*

Stranraer

SOLWAY

Carlisle

Whithorn

*Cumbria*

# 5 - *Vikings, Scots, Picts*

The Norsemen sacked the great religious centre of Lindisfarne in 793, and looted Iona in 795. These Vikings were pagans and were renowned for their cruelty and violence. They ravaged through Skye, then sacked

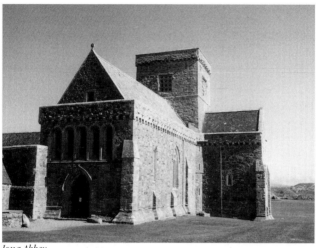

*Iona Abbey*

Iona again in 802 and 806 when they butchered many of the monks. Abbot Cellach of Iona built a new church in 807 for his community at Kells in Ireland (hence the name of the 'Book of Kells'). These continuing attacks eventually forced Iona to be abandoned, and brought terror to all the kingdoms of the north.

In 807 Constantine, son of Fergus, became king of the Picts but his lands were harried relentlessly by the Vikings, particularly Orkney, Shetland and the Outer Hebrides. Constantine also ruled Dalriada from 811. The last of the monks of Iona moved to Dunkeld about this time. Here, encouraged by Constantine, they founded a major ecclesiastical centre. Dunkeld, which is some miles inland, was safer from the attacks of Norse long ships than the island of Iona. The partly ruined cathedral at Dunkeld is built on the site of an earlier church, and some of the relics of St Columba were apparently brought here. Constantine, himself, died in 820, but Viking attacks continued.

The Norsemen raided all along the coasts, and increasingly inland as well, and greatly weakened the kingdoms of Scotland. The Picts could no longer hold their northern lands, and the Vikings settled in Orkney and Shetland, and parts of the mainland and Outer Hebrides, forming a powerful and sometimes chaotic Norse colony.

Angus II, son of Fergus, was king of both Dalriada and of the Picts. By now the Scots and the Picts had had several joint rulers, and there had apparently been much intermarriage between the two peoples, as well as among the Britons. Pictish and Scottish kings were almost interchangeable, and a unification under one dynasty was inevitable – as it would be eventually with the British kingdom of Strathclyde. In 834 there was a major Viking victory over a united army of Picts and Scots. Neither kingdom could stand against the Norsemen alone, and Dalriada, particularly, was vulnerable to attacks from the sea and had been ravaged so often that it was severely weakened, perhaps to the point of final destruction.

Kenneth, son of Alpin, who was born on Iona, was made ruler of

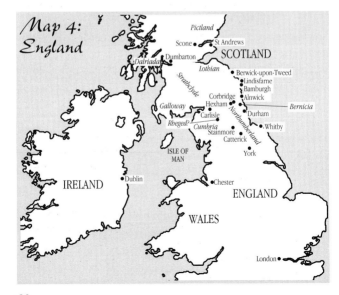

Galloway after his father Alpin had been killed fighting the Picts in 834. Kenneth became king of Dalriada in 840. Brude, son of Feredach, was last king of Picts and died in 843. As Kenneth had a claim to the Pictish throne through his mother, a Pictish princess, there was nothing to bar him from uniting the two peoples.

Kenneth, son of Alpin, the 36th king of Dalriada, became king of the Scots and the Picts in 843. The union seems to have been relatively peaceful, and there do not seem to have been any major battles. Kenneth secured his position, however, by slaughtering all his rivals in a drunken feast at Forteviot – a likely enough event for the time. The site is supposed to be at Halyhill at the west end of the village.

Kenneth brought with him the Stone of Destiny, or Stone of Scone, which is now kept at Edinburgh Castle. There are many legends concerning the Stone of Destiny. One is that it was the pillow of Jacob or of St Columba; while another is that wherever the stone resided the rightful king of Scots would also rule. It was said that St Patrick had blessed the stone, foretelling that the descendants of Erc would reign where the stone was located. Fergus, son of Erc, was the first Dalriadian king, and Kenneth was descended from him. The kings of Dalriada had been inaugurated at Dunadd; but the Pictish kings were enthroned at the Moot Hill at Scone. Scone Palace stands on the site of the abbey, which itself stood on the site of an ancient residence of the early kings. Kenneth also moved from his western strongholds to Dunkeld, Scone, Abernethy, Dunfermline and Forteviot, which were much safer from Viking attack.

The culture and language of the Picts was all to disappear: Gaelic was the language of the kings and of the Columban clergy who gained a resurgence in strength from the union. The court, however, was established in Pictish territory and indeed the old power-base of Dalriada was soon lost to the Vikings. The Picts enduring legacy was their magnificent and enigmatic carved stones.

Kenneth invaded Northumberland on six separate occasions in an attempt to exert his influence to the south, during which he burned both Melrose and Dunbar. He also had to continue to defend the united kingdoms against Viking raids, which on one occasion devastated the country as far as Dunkeld, as well as invasions from the

Strathclyde Britons.

Kenneth I died in 859, and Donald I, Kenneth's brother, succeeded to the throne. It was during his brief reign that the laws of Dalriada were brought together and recorded at Forteviot. Donald's reign was relatively free from Viking raids, but he did not hold the throne for long as he died at Scone in 863 – having probably been murdered.

He was followed by Constantine I, who spent most of his energy – as would so many of his successors – fighting off Viking incursions and trying to extend his influence to the south. The kingdom was raided in 864 by Norsemen under Olaf the White, king of Dublin. The Vikings now employed a new tactic, staying in the area for some months and taking hostages to raise monies in ransom. Constantine defeated and slew Thorsten the Red, another raiding Viking, in 875. The Vikings were still pagans, and churchmen were prey to their murder. St Adrian, who is said to have come from Hungary, settled in the east of Fife along with St Monan. St Monan was killed by invading Vikings and Adrian took refuge on the Isle of May, an island in the Firth of Forth, some four miles south of Fife. He too was slain by the Norsemen in about 870. The island was later used as a priory and was a place of pilgrimage.

Yet kin strife continued, even in the face of devastation at the hands of the Vikings. In 872 Constantine was responsible for the murder of Rhun, king of Strathclyde, who was married to one of his sisters.

Constantine I was eventually slain in battle against the Norsemen in 877, reputedly by a group known as the Black Strangers, who had been driven from Ireland and had established themselves in Fife. Constantine is said to have been killed in the Black Cave near Crail in Fife.

During his reign the Danes had conquered Northumbria. Olaf the White campaigned against the Picts in 866-9, and he and Ivar, king of Dublin, sacked Dumbarton in 870-1, and then used the stronghold as a headquarters to pillage the surrounding area. An army of Vikings defeated a Scots force at Dollar in 877.

Aed, son of Kenneth I and Constantine's younger brother, was made king, but then killed in 878 by his cousin Giric. Giric, son of Donald I – who is also known as Grig – then ruled as joint – or more likely rival – king along with Eochaid of Strathclyde. Eochaid was king of Strathclyde, and son of one of Kenneth I's daughters and Rhun, who had been murdered by Constantine I. Eochaid launched a successful invasion of Northumberland, which led to the kingdom of Scots controlling lands to the south for a time: but the success was short lived. Both kings were deposed: Eochaid died in 889, and Giric was killed in a siege at the fortress of Dundurn. Giric is known as the 'Liberator of the Scottish Church', and is sometimes called the Scottish 'Gregory the Great'. This is said to be due to his releasing the church from the burden of paying duties and dues to secular lords.

The kings who followed were descended from two rival branches: the successors of Constantine I and of Aed (who were both sons of Kenneth I).

Donald II, Constantine I's son, came to the throne, but he was probably poisoned in 900, either near Forres or at Dunnottar. It was from about this time that the Scots increasingly controlled the kingdom of Strathclyde, and it became dependant on the Scots. The British aristocracy of Strathclyde withdrew to the north of Wales.

The kingdom of Scots was still subject to continual raiding and incursions by the Vikings. The Danish leader Guthrum captured Northumberland, while the north of Scotland was seized by Sigurd the Mighty. Even Dunnottar, which would have been virtually impregnable at the time, fell to the Vikings. Unfortunately for Sigurd, he tied the severed head of one of his enemies to his saddle. As he rode along, the severed head bit his leg and Sigurd eventually died of blood poisoning.

*Dunnottar Castle*

# 6 - Kin Strife and Wars

Constantine II, the eldest son of Aed, came to the throne in 900 and ruled for 43 years, a very long reign indeed for the time. The kingdom of Strathclyde was increasingly subject to the Scots, and in 908 the throne passed to Constantine's brother, Donald, while Owen, son of Donald, the latter's son, was king of Strathclyde from 916.

Constantine spent much of his reign fighting the Vikings, the grandsons of Ivar, who plundered the kingdom from the north, marauding down as far as Dunkeld in 903. Constantine drove them

*Bamburgh Castle*

from his realm and slew Ivar in Strathearn the following year.

Vikings under Rognvald attacked Northumberland and forced its ruler Ealdred to abandon his fortress of Bamburgh. Ealdred sought refuge with Constantine, while other Norsemen harried the coasts of Yorkshire. In an attempt to break their power, Constantine attacked the Vikings, and managed to seize Lothian, which he controlled for many years. In 914 the Scots, under Constantine, and Northumbrians, led by Ealdred, brought Rognvald to battle at Corbridge, and there was a second battle in 918. Although both sides claimed victory, Constantine withdrew and returned to his own kingdom.

In 920 Constantine, Rognvald, Ealdred and Owen, king of Strathclyde, chose the Anglo-Saxon king Edward the Elder 'for father and lord' in an attempt to establish a peace, however uneasy. They entered into a treaty with Edward as the Danes under Rognvald were now firmly established in York.

By 927 Rognvald was dead and Athelstan, king of Wessex, had taken York, threatening the borders of the kingdom of Scots and Northumberland. Constantine and Ealdred made peace with Athelstan in 927. The peace lasted until 934 when Athelstan invaded Scotland, reaching as far as Dunnottar and took Constantine's son as hostage before he would withdraw. Constantine seems deliberately to have avoided battle, perhaps because his own forces could not be gathered quickly enough to defeat the English or perhaps because his kingdom was simply not strong enough to resist.

Constantine had had enough, and in 937 the Scots, and an army of Irish and Northumbrian Norsemen under Olaf Gothfrithsson, and Britons, led by Owen of Strathclyde, marched south. They were brought to battle at Brunanburgh and there were routed by Athelstan, with a great slaughter of the Scots and their allies – the events related in the Anglo-Saxon Chronicle. Constantine's son was among the slain, as was Owen of Strathclyde. Strathclyde was harried and the Britons lost control of the lands south of the Solway. The location of this battle has been sited at Burnswark or Birrenswark in Dumfriesshire. Athelstan installed Eric Bloodaxe as earl of Northumberland and Constantine's influence over Strathclyde and Lothian was severely diminished.

The southern borders of the kingdom of Scots were attacked, as Viking raiders marauded along the coasts and sacked Dunbar and St Baldred's church at Tyninghame. In 943 Constantine resigned (he may have had no choice in the matter) his throne to his cousin, Malcolm I, and retired to the monastery at St Andrews, where he died in 952.

Malcolm I, son of Donald II, Constantine's cousin and apparently his preferred choice, came to the throne in 943. Malcolm I is believed to have been responsible for uniting the Pictish and Scottish churches under Cellach, bishop of St Andrews. St Columba's relics were transferred from Dunkeld to St Andrews – if they had not been moved there already.

On coming to the throne Malcolm immediately launched an attack on Moray, where he killed the local king and brought the area under his control. In return for land Malcolm helped Athelstan in his battles against the Norsemen.

In 945 Edmund, successor of Athelstan, invaded Cumbria and granted it to Malcolm, although Edmund was assassinated in 946. Two years later Malcolm plundered the English as far as the Tees taking men and cattle, and in 950 Malcolm captured Northumberland. The men of Moray took the opportunity to rise in rebellion. Malcolm hurried north, but he was killed in battle in 954, possibly at Fetteresso or at Fordoun in the Mearns. The English king Eadred, successor to Edmund, then retook Northumberland and the English controlled York from the same year: Eric Bloodaxe was slain at Stainmore.

The next king was Indulf, son of Constantine II. Although raiding and fighting continued, it was at the beginning of his reign that the Scots captured and held Edinburgh and seized Lothian. Indulf was killed about 962, and is said to have been slain by Vikings driven out of York. One account relates the location of his death as the mouth of a river, either the Cullen in Banffshire or the Cowie, near Dunnottar, in the

*Edinburgh Castle*

Mearns. An alternative site for his death is St Andrews.

Duff the Black, son of Malcolm I, contested the throne with Culen the Whelp, who was Indulf's son. Duff was initially successful and put down a rising in Atholl, slaying the bishop of Dunkeld and the mormaer (a ruler or lesser king) of Atholl. He did not enjoy his throne for long: he was treacherously slain in 967 by the governor of Forres Castle in Moray: it is said that his body was hidden in a deep pool near the castle. The sun would not shine on the spot until his body was found and buried: or so the story goes.

Culen then came to the throne, and tried to re-establish control over the kingdom of Strathclyde. He slew the brother of king Rhiderch, son of Donald, of Strathclyde and captured his daughter. He, too, was not to have a long reign: Rhiderch had his revenge in 971 – Culen and his brother were slain by the Britons in Lothian.

The reign of Kenneth II, brother of Duff, was relatively peaceful. He soon abandoned attempts to avenge his brother's death after suffering a setback in 972. Rhiderch was succeeded as king of Strathclyde by Malcolm in 973. Kenneth maintained friendly relations with his neighbours, although in 971 he had plundered England, this time as far south as Stainmore. Two years later he entered a treaty with the English King Edgar at Chester, acknowledging Edgar as his overlord and receiving Lothian in return. He further strengthened his position at home by murdering Olaf, brother of Culen, a likely rival to the throne.

Kenneth may have broken the treaty and invaded England in 994. He was defeated by Uhtred, who was made earl of Northumberland by the English King Ethelred II. The Scots lost Lothian (again), while Strathclyde was sorely beset by Ethelred himself.

In 995 Kenneth II was poisoned near Fettercairn, traditionally at Green Castle. The deed was done by Finella, wife of the mormaer of the Mearns, whose son had been murdered by Kenneth. Finella had an elaborate trap built, a statue snared with poisoned crossbows, which was triggered by removing a golden apple. An alternative version is that she simply persuaded Kenneth's own men to murder him – a likely enough event. Needless to say Finella did not come to a happy end.

It is during Kenneth's reign that the thistle traditionally became associated with Scotland. In 973 a Scottish army was camped overnight at Luncarty. The Scots were only saved from the Vikings when the Norsemen stumbled into a patch of thistles. The first recorded use of the thistle, however, was in 1470.

Constantine III, son of Aed, came to the throne in 995 after the death of Kenneth II, but was murdered himself two years later by the future Kenneth III. Malcolm, son of Donald, king of Strathclyde also died in 997. Kenneth III, Kenneth the Brown, seized the throne, but he was – in turn – slain in 1005 by Malcolm II, reputedly at Monzievaird, near the River Earn. Kenneth III's son Giric was killed with him. Kenneth had led a disastrous raid into England, and in retaliation the English King Ethelred wrested Lothian (yet again) from the Scots, and in 1000 devastated Strathclyde.

Dynastic fighting, failed invasions, and Norse raids had weakened the kingdom of Scots, and by 1005 the Scots had lost control of Lothian and Strathclyde, the north and west were held by the Norsemen, and Moray and other areas of the north were in open rebellion.

DUNCAN, I.

*Duncan*

# 7 – Duncan, Macbeth and Malcolm Canmore

Malcolm II was proclaimed king in 1005. The beginning of his reign was not auspicious for the Scots: the following year he led an unsuccessful raid into England, reaching Durham, which he besieged in an attempt to seize the relics of St Cuthbert. There he was driven back by Uhtred of Northumbria and forced to retreat – Lothian remained in the possession of the English.

Malcolm turned to the north, and yet again it seemed as if things would go badly: his forces were defeated in 1008 near Forres. In 1010, however, he managed to defeat a Norse army at Dufftown and secured his northern border. This was achieved by a combination of fighting and marrying off his daughter Bethoc to the Norse earl of Orkney, Earl Sigurd the Stout. Incidentally, Sigurd was converted to Christianity in about 995, and from this time Viking paganism declined in Orkney and Shetland. Sigurd's son was Thorfinn the Mighty – Thorfinn Ravenfeeder – earl of Orkney, by Bethoc. Sigurd was defeated and slain at Clontarf in Ireland in 1014.

Turning his attention to the south, Malcolm and the Scots, aided by Owen the Bald of Strathclyde, raised a large army and marched into Lothian. They took advantage of English disarray and weakness, and defeated the English of Northumberland, led by Uhtred, at the battle of Carham in 1018. Their victory gave them command of Lothian. Owen was killed at the battle and Strathclyde was also absorbed into the kingdom of Scots, which now more or less assumed its present southern border. Uhtred hurried south to tell King Canute of his defeat, and Canute had him assassinated, replacing him with his brother Eadalf. Eadalf promptly gave up any claim to Lothian and the territory passed to Malcolm.

Malcolm II appears to have ensured Duncan (his grandson and choice of heir) would succeed to the throne by slaughtering as many other rivals as he could. Duncan was the son of Malcolm's eldest daughter and Crinan, bishop of Dunkeld. Malcolm died on 25 November 1034.

Duncan succeeded to the throne, but his reign was not a success. He unsuccessfully besieged Durham and was twice defeated by Thorfinn, who may have divided the kingdom and ruled the north.

By then Thorfinn controlled Orkney, Shetland, Caithness, Sutherland, and most of the Hebrides, and his power threatened Duncan. Thorfinn made a pilgrimage to Rome and was responsible for building the cathedral on the Brough of Birsay in Orkney. Thorfinn's daughter, Ingioborg, married Malcolm Canmore, and his two sons fought with Harald Hardrada, king of Norway, at Stamford Bridge in 1066 against the English King Harald. The English were victorious, but then went on to defeat at the battle of Hastings against William the Conqueror. Macbeth may have been Thorfinn's half brother, although it is not clear whether they were allies or rivals. Duncan campaigned in Moray and the north, certainly against Thorfinn and possibly against Macbeth.

Duncan was defeated by Thorfinn's forces near Burghead, then was mortally wounded in a battle in 1040 by Macbeth at Spynie near Elgin and died of his wounds – not in his bed with a bloodied dagger as described by Shakespeare, and certainly not at Glamis, Cawdor or Inverness. Macbeth was the son of Finlay, mormaer of Moray and of Donada, daughter of Malcolm II. Macbeth was married to Gruoch, a granddaughter of Kenneth II, and had a son, Lulach, by her first husband (another ruler of Moray). Macbeth ruled well, strengthening the kingdom, and defending himself against Crinan. Crinan was slain in 1045 trying to regain the throne for his grandson Malcolm.

Macbeth felt sufficiently secure to make a pilgrimage to Rome, where he 'scattered alms like seed corn' in 1050. But it was not to be. Malcolm Canmore, son of Duncan, invaded in 1054 with English help and defeated Macbeth's forces, probably at Dunsinane. On 15 August 1057 Macbeth was killed at Lumphanan. Malcolm Canmore – 'Canmore' means big head – was named Malcolm III. Lulach, Macbeth's stepson and son of Gruoch by her first marriage, was set up as a rival claimant to the throne, but was slain by Malcolm in 1058. Although there would be rebellions in Moray, Malcolm's position was secured.

Malcolm Canmore had been in England during most of the reign of Macbeth. He married Ingioborg, daughter of Earl Thorfinn the Mighty of Orkney, by whom he had several children including a son called

Duncan. Ingioborg died some time before 1068.

In 1066 William the Conqueror defeated Harold and the English at the battle of Hastings in the south of England, and two years later Malcolm married Margaret of England, sister to the Saxon heir to the throne of England. Margaret was a very pious woman and was later made a saint.

*Landing of Queen Margaret at Queensferry*

Malcolm invaded England five times between 1061 and 1069, and was forced to swear allegiance to William the Conqueror and a large army in 1072. Malcolm was treacherously killed at Alnwick on 13 November 1093 when he believed he was accepting the surrender of the castle – the lance on which he was being given the keys was thrust through his eye. He had three sons by Ingioborg, including the future Duncan II, and six by Margaret: Edward (who died from wounds received at Alnwick), Ethelred, Edmund, Edgar, Alexander and David – as well as two daughters, one of whom married Henry I of England. Four of his sons by Margaret would be kings.

Margaret died at Edinburgh Castle soon after Malcolm, and she and Malcolm were buried in Dunfermline Abbey (although they were exhumed during the Reformation and their remains taken to the Continent). Following their deaths, Scotland was once again plunged into dynastic turmoil – but that is another story.

'Avaunt, and quit my sight! Let the earth hide thee!

Thy bones are marrowless, thy blood is cold;

Thou hast no speculation in those eyes

Which thou dost glare with.'

# a Wee Guide to
# Macbeth and
# Early Scotland

## Places of Interest

# Map 5: Places of Interest

SHETLAND

Lerwick •

St Ronan's Church, Rona •

• Jarlshof

ORKNEY

Brough of Birsay • • Gurness

• Kirkwall

LEWIS

Stornoway •

HARRIS

NORTH UIST

RAASAY

• Applecross

SOUTH UIST

SKYE

BARRA

HEBRIDES

Cille Bharra

Burghead •

Groam House • • Forres   Elgin

• Cawdor

Inverness •   Mortlach •   Deer •

Monymusk •

• Urquhart   Lumphanan •   Aberdeen •

Dunnottar •

Finella's Castle •

Brechin •

Aberlemno •

Alyth   Glamis •

Fortingall • Dunkeld •   Meigle • • St Vigeans

LISMORE   Macbeth Exp. • Dunsinane • Dundee

• Dunstaffnage   Scone •

Dunollie •   Perth • • St Andrews

IONA   Forteviot •   Cupar •

Eileach an Naoimh • • Kilmartin   Dundurn • Abernethy

COLONSAY   • Dunadd   Dunblane •   Dunfermline •   • Bass Rock

Keills •   Dumbarton •   Dunimarle • • Culross

MULL

Eilean Mor •   Inchinnan • Abercorn •

Tarbert • Paisley •   • Traprain

ISLAY   St Blane's •   Govan • Glasgow

Kilbirnie •   Edinburgh •

Kildalton •   ARRAN   Vikingar •

BUTE   • Netherton

Holy Island

• Dunaverty

Auld Kirk of Kilbrine *see* Kilbirnie
Green Castle *see* Finella's Castle
Hunterian Museum *see* Glasgow
Museum nan Eilean *see* Stornoway
Museum of Scotland *see* Edinburgh
Orkney Museum *see* Kirkwall
St Ninian's Cave *see* Whithorn
Shetland Museum *see* Lerwick
Sueno's Stone *see* Forres

• Nith Bridge

ENGLAND

Ruthwell •   Hadrian's Wall

Hadrian's Wall

Kirkmadrine • • Whithorn   • Carlisle

# List of Places of Interest

| | |
|---|---|
| Abercorn Church and Museum | 46 |
| Aberdeen Anthropological Museum | 81 |
| Aberlemno Sculpted Stones | 46 |
| Abernethy | 47 |
| Alyth Castle | 81 |
| Antonine Wall | 81 |
| Applecross | 47 |
| Auld Kirk of Kilbirnie | 48 |
| Bass Rock | 48 |
| Brechin Cathedral | 49 |
| Brough of Birsay | 49 |
| Burghead | 50 |
| Cathedral of St Moluag, Lismore | 50 |
| Cawdor Castle | 51 |
| Cille Bharra | 51 |
| Culross Abbey | 52 |
| Cupar Castle | 52 |
| Deer Abbey | 53 |
| Dumbarton Castle | 53 |
| Dunadd | 54 |
| Dunaverty Castle | 54 |
| Dunblane Cathedral | 55 |
| Dundurn | 56 |
| Dunfermline Abbey and Palace | 56 |
| Dunimarle Castle | 57 |
| Dunkeld Cathedral | 57 |
| Dunnottar Castle | 58 |
| Dunollie Castle | 58 |
| Dunsinane Hill | 59 |
| Dunstaffnage Castle | 59 |
| Edinburgh Castle | 60 |
| Eileach an Naoimh | 61 |
| Eilean Mor, South Knapdale | 61 |
| Elgin | 61 |
| Finella's Castle | 62 |
| Forres Castle | 63 |
| Forteviot | 63 |
| Fortingall | 63 |
| Glamis Castle | 64 |
| Glasgow Cathedral | 64 |
| Govan Old Parish Church | 65 |
| Groam House Museum and Pictish Centre, Rosemarkie | 65 |
| Gurness Broch | 66 |
| Holy Island | 66 |
| Hunterian Museum | 82 |
| Inchinnan Early Christian Stones | 67 |
| Inverness Castle | 67 |
| Inverness Museum and Art Gallery | 82 |
| Iona Abbey | 67 |
| Jarlshof | 69 |
| Keills Chapel | 69 |
| Kildalton Cross and Chapel | 70 |
| Kilmartin House Museum | 70 |
| Kirkmadrine Early Christian Stones | 71 |
| Lumphanan | 71 |
| Macbeth Experience – Perthshire Visitor Centre, Bankfoot | 71 |
| Meigle Sculptured Stone Museum | 72 |
| Monymusk Church | 72 |
| Mortlach Parish Church | 73 |
| Museum nan Eilean, Stornoway | 82 |
| Museum of Scotland | 83 |
| Netherton Cross, Hamilton | 73 |
| Nith Bridge Cross Shaft, Thornhill | 73 |
| Orkney Museum | 83 |
| Paisley Abbey | 74 |
| Perth Museum and Art Gallery | 83 |
| Ruthwell Cross | 74 |
| Scone Palace | 74 |
| Shetland Museum | 84 |
| St Andrews Cathedral | 75 |
| St Blane's Church, Kingarth | 76 |
| St Ninian's Cave | 76 |
| St Ronan's Church, Rona | 77 |
| St Vigeans Sculpted Stones | 77 |
| Sueno's Stone, Forres | 78 |
| Tarbert Castle | 78 |
| Traprain Law Fort | 78 |
| Urquhart Castle | 79 |
| Vikingar | 79 |
| Whithorn Priory | 79 |

# Places of Interest

## Abercorn Church and Museum

NT 082792   LR: 65

*Off A904, 2.5 miles W of South Queensferry, Hopetoun Estate.*

There has been a church on the site for 1500 years. Abercorn was one of the first bishoprics in Scotland, dating from 681 AD, and founded as part of the Anglian church of Northumbria. Its bishop was Trumwin, who was to administer the parts of Pictland then under Northumbrian control. It was abandoned four years later after the battle of Nechtansmere. The present church, which is dedicated to St Serf, dates from the 12th century. Viking burial stones.

**Open daily all year.**
Explanatory displays. Disabled access. Car Parking.
**Tel: 0131 331 1869**

## Aberlemno Sculpted Stones

HS   NO 523557   LR: 54

*Off B9134, 6 miles NE of Forfar, Angus.*

A magnificent group of Pictish stones, the most impressive and elaborate of which is the double-sided cross-slab standing in Aberlemno churchyard. The front of the stone carries a full-length cross in high relief, decorated with intricate interlaced designs and surrounded by intertwining animals. The reverse is framed by two serpents, which surround a depiction of a battle, believed to be the battle of Nechtansmere in 685 when the Picts led by Brude, son of Bile, routed a Northumbrian army.

A double-sided cross-slab stands by the roadside in Aberlemno, while about 0.25 miles north of the church, stands another fine carved Pictish stone.

**Accessible all year – stones enclosed for protection from Oct-Apr and cannot be viewed during this time.**
Parking nearby.
**Tel: 0131 668 8800   Fax: 0131 668 8888**

# *Abernethy*

HS  NO 190165  LR: 58

*On A913, 6 miles SE of Perth, Perth & Kinross.*

The imposing round tower is all that remains of an important ecclesiastical site, which is said to have been founded by nuns from Kildare around 625. It was a bishopric until 908 when it was transferred to St Andrews. It is one of only two such Irish-style round towers remaining in Scotland – the other is at Brechin Cathedral. A Pictish stone, discovered in the early 19th century, is now located at the foot of the tower, and four other symbol stones from Abernethy are in the Museum of Scotland.

The remains of a fort, still in use during the Early Historic period, stands on top of the hill overlooking the town.

**Open Apr-Sep – for access apply to key holder.**
Parking nearby.
**Tel: 0131 668 8800   Fax: 0131 668 8888**

# *Applecross*

NG 713458  LR: 24

*Off A896, Applecross, 1 mile N of village, Wester Ross.*

In a picturesque location, this is the site of a Christian monastic community, founded in 673 by St Maelrubha, who was from Bangor in Ireland. The saint died in 722, and he is believed to be buried here. An 8th-century cross-slab

Applecross

stands by the gate into the burial ground, and inside the modern church are a further three fragments. The modern church dates from 1817, but nearby is a ruinous 15th-century chapel – roofed over by a shrub growing up inside the walls.

***Access at all reasonable times.***
Parking nearby.


# Auld Kirk of Kilbirnie

NS 314546   LR: 63

*Off B780, Dalry Road, Kilbirnie, Ayrshire.*

The church, which dates from 1470, stands on the site of a 6th-century monastery of St Brendan of Clonfert. There is fine Italian Renaissance-style carving from 1642.

***Open Jul-Aug, Mon-Fri 14.00-16.00.***
Sales area. WC. Disabled access. Parking nearby.
**Tel: 01505 683459**


# Bass Rock

NT 602873   LR: 67

*A rock in the Firth of Forth, 3 miles NE of North Berwick, East Lothian.*

The Bass, a huge rock in the Firth of Forth, was the hermitage of St Baldred of Tyninghame, a saint who was active among the Angles of Lothian and died here in 756. There are some remains of a chapel dedicated to the saint. The island is home to thousands of seabirds, and is the third largest gannetry in the world. St Baldred also founded a church at Tyninghame [NT 620798], but it was sacked by Vikings in 943.

***Boat trips from North Berwick go around Bass Rock – tel 01620 892838 (boat trips) or 01620 892197 (tourist information office).***
Car parking.
**Tel: 01620 892838**

# Brechin Cathedral

NO 596601   LR: 44

*Off A935, Brechin, Angus.*

The cathedral dates from the 13th century, and nearby is an Irish-style round tower from an earlier establishment, dating from the 10th or 11th century. Only two of these towers survive in Scotland, the other being at Abernethy. The cathedral houses a Pictish cross-slab, with a ringed cross, figures and interlaced design.

**Open all year.**
Sales area. Parking nearby.

*Round tower, Brechin Cathedral*

# Brough of Birsay

HS   NY 239285   LR: 6

*Tidal island, 20 miles NW of Kirkwall, Orkney*

On a tidal island, the Brough of Birsay, are the remains of a settlement, dating from early times, which was an important place in the Viking period.

A fine Pictish sculptured stone, decorated with figures, was found on the islet. The original is now in the Museum of Scotland, and was replaced by a replica. Thorfinn the Mighty, earl of Orkney – who was also known as Thorfinn Ravenfeeder – held the northern isles, Hebrides and Caithness and Sutherland, and had a hall here. There was a substantial church, consisting of a rectangular nave, smaller chancel and an apse. There are also the foundations of an enclosure wall, and several other buildings. The island is reached by a causeway, which floods at high tide.

**Open all year – check tides as causeway floods.**
Parking nearby.
**Tel: 0131 668 8800   Fax: 0131 668 8888**

# Burghead

NJ 110690   LR: 28

*Off B9089, 8 miles NW of Elgin, Burghead, Moray.*

Burghead was one of the major centres of the Picts, and was a splendid example of a fortification, with three 800-foot long ramparts. Fine Pictish carved stones were found here, many decorated with bulls, which can now been seen in the Burghead Library, Elgin Museum, Museum of Scotland and British Museum in London. Unfortunately most of the fort was destroyed with the building of the present village.

The fort was built between the 4th and 6th centuries, and was destroyed some 500 years later, although it was sufficiently intact to be used as a base by Thorfinn Ravenfeeder, earl of Orkney, in the 11th century. It was nearby that Duncan was defeated by Thorfinn in 1040. Duncan was then slain after a battle with Macbeth near Spynie.

There is a well, once within the fort, which is believed to be early Christian and associated with St Ethan. It consists of a rock-cut chamber, down some stone steps, with a deep tank of water and a basin and pedestal in opposite corners.

**Well (HS): access at all reasonable times.**
Parking nearby.
**Tel: 0131 668 8800   Fax: 0131 668 8888**

# Cathedral of St Moluag, Lismore

NM 860434   LR: 49

*Off B8045, 1.5 miles N of Achnacroish, Clachan, Lismore.*

St Moluag founded a Christian community on the island in the 560s, and is said to have converted parts of Pictland to Christianity. Moluag, who was also from Ireland, and Columba competed as to who would secure the island first, and Moluag cut off his little finger and flung it onto Lismore. The 14th-century cathedral is now much reduced in size although it is still used as the parish church. Several carved slabs, dating from medieval times, survive in the burial ground.

**Parish church.**
Disabled access. Parking nearby.

# Cawdor Castle

NH 847499   LR: 27

*Off B9090, 5 miles SW of Nairn, Highlands.*

The title 'Thane of Cawdor' is associated with Macbeth in Shakespeare's play, but Duncan was not murdered here – the castle is not nearly old enough. In fact, Duncan died in 1040 from wounds received in a battle with Macbeth near Spynie. Nevertheless, Cawdor is one of the most magnificent and well-preserved strongholds in Scotland, and is well worth a visit.

**Open May-mid-Oct daily 10.00-17.30; last admission 17.00.**
Fine collections of portraits, furnishings and tapestries. Explanatory displays. Three shops: gift shop, wool and book shop. Licensed restaurant and snack bar. Gardens, grounds and nature trails. Golf course and putting. Disabled access to grounds; some of castle. Car and coach parking. Group concessions. Conferences. £££.
**Tel: 01667 404615**
 **Fax: 01667 404674**
**Email: cawdor.castle@btinternet.com**

# Cille Bharra

NF 704077   LR: 31

*Off A888, 6 miles N of Castlebay, Eoligarry, N end of Barra.*

The present ruinous medieval church dates from the 12th century and was dedicated to St Barr, a saint who converted the folk of Barra to Christianity (and dissuaded them from cannibalism – or so the story goes). There was also a fine carved stone, dating from the 10th or 11th century, with a cross and inscription which reads: 'after Thorgerth, Steiner's daughter, this cross was raised'. The original is now kept in the Museum of Scotland: a replica is kept at Cille Bharra. Two chapels also survive: one has been rerooted to shelter several carved slabs, and there are other slabs in the burial ground.

***Access at all times.***
Parking nearby.

# Culross Abbey

HS   NS 989863   LR: 63

*Off B9037, Kirk Street, Culross, Fife.*

Situated in the pretty white-washed village of Culross, the abbey here was dedicated to St Serf and St Mary, and founded in 1217 by Malcolm, earl of Fife. It was at Culross that St Enoch (daughter of the king of Lothian) came in the 6th century, bearing St Mungo or Kentigern. Mungo was educated by St Serf, and went on to convert the Britons of Strathclyde to Christianity. He founded Glasgow Cathedral in 573, where he is buried.

  Culross Abbey became ruinous after the Reformation, except for the choir, which has been used as the parish church since 1633. There are the fragments of three cross shafts near the church, dating from the 8th or 9th century. The remains of the domestic buildings are open to the public. Also in the village is Culross Palace, the well-preserved 16th- and 17th-century residence of Sir George Bruce.

***Open all year at reasonable times.***
WC. Sales area. Disabled access. Parking Nearby.
**Tel: 0131 668 8800   Fax: 0131 668 888**

# Cupar Castle

NO 374146   LR: 59

*Off A91, Cupar, Castlehill, Fife.*

One tale sets a stronghold in Cupar as the place where Lady MacDuff and her babes were butchered by Macbeth's assassins, but Dunimarle is a more popular location – if such an event ever took place. There was a castle here, which was held by the MacDuff Earls of Fife, and the court of the Stewarty of Fife was held here until 1425.

# *Deer Abbey*

HS   NJ 968482   LR: 30

*Off A950, 2 miles W of Mintlaw, Aberdeenshire.*

Deer is associated with St Drostan, a nephew of St Columba, and he founded a monastic settlement here. The beautifully illustrated 11th- or 12th-century Book of Deer was produced at the monastery, but is now in the library of Cambridge University. The present ruinous abbey was founded in 1219 by William Comyn, earl of Buchan.

**Open at all reasonable times.**
Parking.
**Tel: 0131 668 8800   Fax: 0131 668 8888**

# *Dumbarton Castle*

HS   NS 400745   LR: 64

*Off A814, in Dumbarton.*

Standing on a commanding rock on the north shore of the Clyde, Dumbarton or 'Al Cluith' was the main fortress of the British kingdom of Strathclyde from the 5th century or earlier – indeed the name means 'fortress of the Britons'. In 756 it was captured by Picts and Northumbrians, and in 870 was besieged by Irish raiders, who captured the rock only after four months of fighting, starving the garrison into surrender. Owen the Bald, the last king of Strathclyde, died at the battle of Carham in 1018, and Strathclyde was absorbed into the kingdom of Scots.

  Dumbarton became a royal castle, and was a formidable fortress, and saw much action down the centuries – although little remains from the early period. Exhibition in Governor's House.

**Open daily all year: Apr-Sep daily 9.30-18.30; Oct-Mar Mon-Sat 9.30-16.30 except closed Thu PM & Fri, Sun 14.00-16.30; closed 25/26 Dec & 1-3 Jan.**
Exhibitions.Gift shop. WC. Car Parking. Group concessions. £.
**Tel: 01389 732167**

# Dunadd

HS NR 836936 LR: 55

*Off A816, 3.5 miles S of Kilmartin, Dunadd, Argyll.*

Commanding fine views, Dunadd dates from 100 AD, and consists of lines of fortifications, some well preserved, and the well-defined entrance. This was a stronghold of the Scots, after they first arrived from Ireland from the 3rd

century, and St Columba ordained Aedan, son of Gabhrain, the sixth king of the Dalriadian Scots here. The inauguration appears to have involved the basin and footprint carved in a rock towards the summit. The Stone of Destiny was kept here until taken to Scone by Kenneth I. In the Annals of Ulster it is recorded that Dunadd was besieged and captured by the Picts in 683 and 736. The fort was abandoned in the 10th century.

**Open all year.**
Parking nearby.

# Dunaverty Castle

NR 688074 LR: 68

*Off B842, 8 miles S of Campbeltown, Dunaverty, Argyll.*

On a steep promontory above the sea, this was one of the strongholds of the

Scottish kingdom of Dalriada, and was captured and burnt. It was reused as a medieval castle, but little now remains.

***Access at all reasoable times – care should be taken.***

# *Dunblane Cathedral*

HS   NN 782015   LR: 57

*Off B8033, Dunblane, Stirlingshire.*

Set in the picturesque town of Dunblane by the banks of the Allen River, the cathedral is dedicated to St Blane and built on the site of an ecclesiastical centre

dating from Pictish times. Housed in the building is a 9th-century ringed cross-slab with two serpent heads, as well as another carved stone. The oldest part of the cathedral is the pre-13th-century bell-tower, and it is still used as the parish church.

***Open all year.***
Sales area. WC. Disabled access. Parking nearby.
**Tel: 01786 823338**

# Dundurn

NN 708233   LR: 51

*Off A85, 4 miles W of Comrie, Dundurn fort, Perthshire.*

The remains of an Iron Age fort or early castle, which was a major stronghold of the Picts, but was attacked in 683. Giric, kings of Scots was slain here during a siege in 889.

# Dunfermline Abbey and Palace

HS   NT 089872   LR: 65

*Off A994, in Dunfermline, Fife.*

Dunfermline was an important Pictish and religious site. The abbey was founded about 1070 by Margaret, wife of Malcolm Canmore, as a Benedictine house on the site of an older Christian site. Margaret was made a saint, and she and Malcolm were buried here in 1093. Abbot George Durie, the last abbot at the time of the Reformation, was responsible for removing their remains to the continent, where the Jesuits of Douai in Spain secured Margaret's head.

  Robert the Bruce's body (apart from his heart) is buried here. The Abbey was sacked in 1560, and fell into disrepair, although part of the church continued to be used, and it was rebuilt in modern times.  The church, domestic buildings of

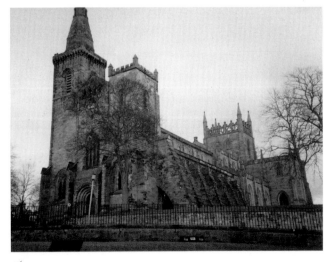

the abbey, and the remains of the Royal Palace are open to the public.

Nearby in Pittencrieff Park is Malcolm Canmore's Tower [NT 088873], traditionally believed to have been built by Malcolm, although the existing, very ruinous remains appear to date from not earlier than the 14th century.

*Open all year: Apr-Sep daily 9.30-18.30; Oct-Mar, Mon-Sat 9.30-16.30 except closed Thu PM and Fri, Sun 14.00-16.30; choir of abbey church closed winter.*

Exhibition. Giftshop. Parking nearby. Group concessions. &.

**Tel: 01383 739026**

# *Dunimarle Castle*

NS 978859   LR: 65

*Off B9037, 1 mile W of Culross, Dunimarle, Fife.*

The castle is built on the traditional site of the murder of Lady MacDuff and her children, as related in Shakespeare's *Macbeth*. The property was later held by the Erskines, and a collection of furniture and other items from the castle are currently on display at Duff House, near Banff, which is under the guardianship of Historic Scotland. Dunimarle is not open to the public.

# *Dunkeld Cathedral*

HS   NO 025426   LR: 52

*Off A923, Dunkeld, Perthshire.*

Standing in the scenic village of Dunkeld on the banks of the Tay, part of the 14th-century cathedral is still used as the parish church, although the nave is now ruinous. The 15th-century chapter house has a small museum. The tower, ruined nave and south porch are in the care of Historic Scotland. Some of the relics of St Columba were brought here after Iona was abandoned, and it was a major religious centre from Pictish times.

To the east of Dunkeld is Birnam, from where – in Shakespeare's play *Macbeth* – the wood is said to have travelled the twelve miles to Dunsinane Hill. A fort to the south of Dunkeld [NO 046392] is known as 'Duncan's Camp'.

*Ruined nave and tower access at all reasonable times; choir used as parish church: open  summer 9.30-19.00; winter 9.30-16.00.*

Museum. Picnic area. Parking nearby.

**Tel: 0131 668 8800   Fax: 0131 668 8888**

# Dunnottar Castle

NO 882839  LR: 45

*Off A92, 2 miles S of Stonehaven, Kincardine & Deeside.*

Built on a promontory on cliffs high above the sea, Dunnottar Castle is a spectacular ruined courtyard castle of the Keith earls Marischal. The site is particularly strong and was used by the Picts and Scots as a stronghold. Donald II was probably poisoned here in 900, and it was soon captured by the Vikings. Athelstan, king of the English invaded Scotland, and reached Dunnottar in 943. Getting to the castle involves a walk, steep climb, and a steeper one back.

**Open Easter-Oct Mon-Sat 9.00-18.00, Sun 14.00-17.00; winter Mon-Fri only 09.00 to sunset.**

Getting to the castle involves a walk, steep climb, and a steeper one back. Sales area. WC. Car and coach parking. Group concessions. Parking. &.

**Tel: 01569 762173**

# Dunollie Castle

NM 852314  LR: 49

*Off A85, 1 mile N of Oban, Dunollie, Argyll.*

Standing on a rocky ridge overlooking the sea, Dunollie is a ruined and overgrown castle of the MacDougalls. In 698 Dunollie, then a fortress of the kings of Dalriada, was captured and destroyed. The castle, which may be in a dangerous condition, can be reached from a lay-by on the Ganavan road, but not from the drive to Dunollie House, which is not open to the public.

# Dunsinane Hill

NO 214316   LR: 53

*Off B953, 7 miles NE of Perth, Dunsinane, Perthshire.*

The summit of Dunsinane Hill is surrounded by lines of defences, and a souterrain was found within the fort. The fort is known as 'Macbeth's Castle' and is traditionally where Macbeth awaited the forces of Malcolm Canmore and most of Birnam Wood (which, although some twelve miles away can be seen from the summit). According to the play, Macbeth was killed at the subsequent battle here – but although it is likely that Macbeth was defeated here in 1054, it was not until 1057 that he was slain, and that was at Lumphanan.

About two miles to the north is another site [NO 201344] associated with Macbeth – 'Macbeth's Law' – which is a large mound and may be a prehistoric burial cairn.

# Dunstaffnage Castle

HS   NM 882344   LR: 49

*Off A85, 3.5 miles NE of Oban, Argyll.*

On a promontory in the Firth of Lorn, Dunstaffnage consists of a massive 13th-century castle of the MacDougalls. A stronghold here was held by the kings of

Dalriada in the 7th century, and was one of the places that the Stone of Destiny was kept.

**Open daily Apr-Sep 9.00-18.00; Oct-Mar Mon-Sat 9.00-16.00, Sun 14.00-16.30, except closed Thu PM and Fri; last ticket 30 mins before closing.**
Explanatory panels. Gift shop. WC. Car and coach parking. Group concessions. &.
**Tel: 01631 562465**

# Edinburgh Castle

HS   NT 252735   LR: 66

*Off A1, in the centre of Edinburgh.*

Standing on a high rock, Edinburgh Castle was one of the strongest and most important fortresses in Scotland. The rock had been used as a stronghold by the Britons of Lothian, but Lothian was seized by the Angles of Northumberland in 638 and Edinburgh captured. Edinburgh was taken by the Scots in the 10th century, but it was not until after the battle of Carham in 1018 that Lothian and Edinburgh were ceded to the kings of Scots. Margaret, wife of Malcolm Canmore, died here in 1093 and the oldest building of the castle is a small charming Norman chapel of the early 12th century, which is dedicated to her.

The rock was used as the site for a medieval castle and remained one of the most important strongholds in the country. It is now home to the Scottish crown jewels, and the Stone of Destiny – on which the kings of Scots were inaugurated at Dunadd and Scone – and is an interesting complex of buildings with spectacular views over the capital. Scottish War Memorial. Visitors with a disability can be taken to the top of the castle by a courtesy vehicle; ramps and lift access to Crown Jewels and Stone of Destiny. Disabled facilities and WC.

**Open daily all year: Apr-Sep 9.30-17.15; Oct-Mar 9.30-16.15, castle closes 45 mins after last ticket is sold; times may be altered during Tattoo and state occasions; closed Christmas & New Year.**
Explanatory displays. Guided tours. Gift shop. Restaurant. WC. Disabled access. Visitors with a disability can be taken to the top of the castle by a courtesy vehicle; ramps and lift access to Crown Jewels and Stone of Destiny. Car and coach parking (except during Tattoo). £££.
**Tel: 0131 225 9846**

# Eileach an Naoimh

HS  NM 640097  LR: 55

*N of Jura, one of the Garvellach islands.*

St Brendan of Clonfert founded an early Christian community here in 542, predating St Columba's arrival on Iona by some twenty years. There are the ruins of beehive cells as well as two churches within an enclosure and two burial grounds. This is the traditional burial place of Eithne, St Columba's mother, which is marked by a round setting of stones. One small slab is decorated with an early cross, and it is said that when the grave was opened the remains of a woman were discovered.

The island can be reached by hired boat from Toberonochy, Luing, weather permitting.

**Access at all times – subject to weather.**
**Tel: 0131 668 8800   Fax 0131 668 8888**

# Eilean Mor, South Knapdale

NR 665755  LR: 61

*2 miles W of the mainland at Kilmory, Eilean Mor.*

Standing on an island are several sites associated with St Cormac. The remains of a chapel [NR 666752] with a barrel-vaulted chancel survive, although the building was being used as an inn around 1600. The chapel was dedicated about 640 to St Cormac, although it appears to date from the 13th century. There is a stone effigy of a priest preserved in the chapel. St Cormac is reputedly buried on the island, a broken and weathered cross marking the spot [NR 667753]. The cross is decorated with interlace patterns and representations of animals and people. A cave Uamh nam Fear [NR 666750] is also associated with the saint, and one of the walls has an early Christian cross.

# Elgin

NJ 212628  LR: 28

*Off A96, Elgin, Ladyhill, Moray.*

Duncan is said to have died at a stronghold here in 1040 from wounds inflicted by Macbeth. Not much remains of a later castle, but there are excellent views

from the top of
Ladyhill.

Also in Elgin is the
fine ruinous 13th-
century cathedral,
which is open to the
public. There is a
fine Pictish cross-
slab, the large stone
effigy of a bishop, a
carved grave slab
and an interesting
burial ground, as
well as the well-
preserved chapter
house.

***Castle: access at
all reasonable
times; cathedral: open all year, Apr-Sep daily 9.30-18.30; Oct-Mar,
Mon-Sat 9.30-16.30 except closed ThuPM and Fri, Sun 14.00-16.30.***
Explanatory panels and exhibition. Sales area. Limited disabled access. Car and
coach parking nearby. Group concessions. &.
**Tel: 01343 547171**

## Finella's Castle

NO 633723   LR: 45

*Off B966, 1 mile SW of Fettercairn, Cairnton of Balbegno, at Finella's Castle
(Green Castle), Kincardine and Deeside.*

Situated on the top of a rise, Finella's Castle is an Iron Age fort, and consists of
two enclosing walls, the ground sloping steeply away on three sides.

   This was the stronghold where – reputedly – Finella, wife of the mormaer of
the Mearns, murdered Kenneth III in 994. Kenneth slew her son, and she built
an elaborate statue, trapped with bolts, which was activated when the king
removed an apple from the contraption, and so he was slain. She also died, for
her pains, reputedly in the Den of Finella, at St Cyrus. An alternative story is
that she simply persuaded Kenneth's men to murder him, which – given the
record of the kings of Scots in the 9th and 10th centuries – was probably not
too difficult.

# Forres Castle

NJ 035588   LR: 27

*Off B9011, Forres, Moray.*

This was the site of the murder of King Duff in 966. He is said to have been slain by the governor of the castle, who concealed his body in a deep pool, but until it was found the sun would not shine on the spot. Little remained of the castle by the mid 18th century, and the site is now a public park.

About four miles to the east and just north of the A96 is 'Macbeth's Hillock', said to be where Macbeth and Banquo met the witches.

**Access at all reasonable times.**
Parking nearby.

# Forteviot

NN 053176   LR: 58

*On B935, 4.5 miles SW of Perth, Forteviot, Perthshire.*

Forteviot was the site of a palace and centre of the Pictish kings. The site was traditionally at Halyhill to the west of the village, and it is here that Kenneth I slaughtered his rivals at a drunken feast. A church existed at Forteviot from the 8th century, on the site of which stands the present parish church. A bronze bell, dated 900 AD, is preserved here, and there are medieval carved stones.

**Church open by arrangement: tel 01738 625854.**

# Fortingall

NN 736470   LR: 52

*Off B846, 5 miles W of Aberfeldy, Perthshire.*

Fortingall is reputed to be the birthplace of Pontius Pilate, the son of a Roman emissary and a local girl. In the churchyard is a 3000-year-old yew tree, and in the church itself a bell said to have been used by St Adamnan, biographer of St Columba, and a 7th-century font. Fortingall, a picturesque village with thatched cottages, was a religious centre from the 6th century.

**Access to churchyard at all reasonable times.**
Car parking.

# Glamis Castle

NO 387481  LR: 54

*Off A928, 5.5 miles SW of Forfar, Angus.*

One of the most famous and magnificent castles in Scotland, Glamis Castle consists of a greatly extended 14th-century keep, set in an extensive park. Malcolm II is said to have died here in 1034, and Glamis is traditionally associated with Macbeth. In the old keep is 'Duncan's Hall', but any connection is probably only from Shakespeare's play. The castle is home to the Lyon, Earls of Strathmore and Kinghorne, and the present Queen Mother comes from this family.

**Open 27 Mar-31 Oct 10.30-17.30 (from 10.00 Jul & Aug); last tour 16.45; at other time groups by appt.**
Collections of historic pictures, porcelain and furniture. Guided tours. Two additional exhibition rooms. Four shops. Licensed restaurant. WC. Picnic area. Play park. Garden. Nature trail. Disabled access to gardens and ground floor; WC. Car and coach parking. Group concessions. £££.
**Tel: 01307 840393   Fax: 01307 840733**

# Glasgow Cathedral

HS   NS 602655   LR: 64

*Castle Street, centre of Glasgow.*

Dedicated to St Mungo (who is also known as St Kentigern), Glasgow's patron saint, the present building is the only medieval cathedral in mainland Scotland to survive the Reformation complete. The cathedral is

believed to have been founded by St Mungo in 573 and is built over his tomb. The building has a fine crypt, and a 15th-century stone screen.

***Open all year Apr-Sep Mon-Sat 9.30-18.30, Sun 14.00-18.30; Oct-Mar Mon-Sat 9.30-16.30, Sun 14.00-16.30; closed 25/26 Dec & 1-3 Jan.***
Gift shop. Parking nearby.
**Tel: 0141 552 6891**

# Govan Old Parish Church

NS 553658   LR: 64

*Off A739, 866 Govan Road, Govan, Glasgow.*

The church houses a fine collection of early Christian stones, including a decorated sarcophagus, five hogback (Viking) tombstones, two cross shafts and upright crosses, and a number of other slabs.

***Open by arrangement only.***
Sales area. WC. Parking nearby.
**Tel: 0141 445 1941**

# Groam House Museum and Pictish Centre, Rosemarkie

*On A832, 1 mile NE of Fortrose, High Street, Rosemarkie, Ross and Cromarty.*

Rosemarkie was a major ecclesiastical centre in early Christian times. This award-winning museum holds fifteen sculpted stones, all found within the village. The most impressive is the Rosemarkie Cross, a magnificent, intricately carved stone. The museum also features audio-visual and static displays, activities and temporary exhibitions.

***Open Easter week, then May-Sep, Mon-Sat 10.00-17.00, Sun 14.00-16.30; Oct-Apr Sat & Sun 14.00-16.00 – admission free (Oct-Apr).***
Guided tours on request. Exhibitions. Gift Shop. Disabled limited access and WC. Car and coach parking. Group concessions. £.
**Tel: 01381 620961**

# Gurness Broch

HS   HY 381268   LR: 6

*Off A966, 1 mile NE of Evie, Gurness, Orkney.*

Excavated in the 1930s, Gurness is a good example of a broch and its surrounding settlement. The settlement was occupied by the Picts, and a stone carved with Pictish devices was found here. There is a museum at the site. Walk to broch.

**Open Apr-Sep, daily 9.30-18.30; last ticket 30 mins before closing – combined ticket available for Orkney monuments.**
Explanatory displays. Disabled access. Car and limited coach parking. Group concession. &.
**Tel: 01831 579478**

# Holy Island

NS 052308   LR: 69

*NW of Holy Island, Arran.*

In the 7th century St Molaise, who was born in Dalriada and educated in Ireland, founded a monastery here. A cave [NS 053303], known as the Smugglers' Cave, is inscribed with several crosses. The island is now home to a Buddhist retreat and centre.

# Inchinnan Early Christian Stones

NS 479689  LR: 64

*Off A8, Inchinnan, Renfrew.*

Inchinnan was an early Christian site, and was dedicated to St Conval, a saint from Ireland. A carved sarcophagus, grave-slab and cross-slab are located in a covered area between the church and bell-tower. The present church was built when the old medieval church was demolished to make way for Glasgow airport.

**Open all year.**
Disabled access. Parking.

# Inverness Castle

NH 667451  LR: 26

*Off A82, Inverness, Highlands.*

Inverness was strategically important, and the Picts had a major stronghold here. After seeing much action, it was finally captured and blown up by the Jacobites in 1746 after the battle of Culloden. A mock castle of 1835 was built on the site, and part of it houses a small exhibition.

  Malcolm Canmore is said to have destroyed a castle of Macbeth (known handily enough as 'Macbeth's Castle') at Inverness in 1057 – the site may have been about 0.5 miles east of the town [NH 673 455], where there were some remains of a stronghold in the 17th century. The site is now occupied by houses. Duncan is said to have been buried at Culcabock [NH 684446], but it is believed he was actually buried on Iona.

**Exhibition open in summer.**
Parking nearby.

# Iona Abbey

NM 287245  LR: 48

*Off A849, Iona, Argyll.*

Situated on the lovely, peaceful island of Iona, this is where St Columba came from Ireland to form a monastic community, and converted the Picts of northern Scotland to Christianity. He died in 597, and Columba's shrine, within

the Abbey buildings, dates from the 9th century. The magnificent 8th-century St Martin's Cross and St John's Cross – the latter a replica – stand just outside the church, and the museum houses a splendid collection of sculptured stones and crosses, one of the largest collections of early Christian carved stones in Europe. Many of the early Kings of Scots are buried in 'Reilig Odhrain' – the 'Street of the Dead' – as well as kings of Ireland, France and Norway: 48 Scottish, eight Norwegian and four Irish kings. The 11th-century chapel of St Oran also survives, and may have been built on the orders of Queen Margaret, wife of Malcolm Canmore. Among the kings buried here are both Duncan and Macbeth.

The abbey was abandoned after raids by the Vikings: they slew the abbot and fifteen monks in 986. The abbey was re-established by Queen Margaret, wife of Malcolm Canmore, in the 11th century. Although the buildings became ruinous after the Reformation, the abbey church and cloister were rebuilt from 1910 for the Iona Community, and it is possible to stay at the Abbey.

There is also the Columba centre at Fionnphort, which has displays about the saint and local information about the islands (01681 700660).

### *Open at all times – ferry from Fionnphort (£), no cars on Iona. Walk to abbey.*

Day tours from Oban in summer. Guided tours. Explanatory displays. Gift shop. Tea-room. WC. Car and coach parking at Fionnphort. & (ferry). Week long programmes for guests.

**Tel: 01681 700404   Fax: 01898 840270**
**Email: iona_abbey@compuserve.com**

# *Jarlshof*

HS   HU 398095   LR: 4

*Off A970, Sumburgh Head, 22 miles S of Lerwick, Shetland.*

One of the most remarkable archaeological sites in Europe. There are remains from the Bronze Age, Iron Age, Pictish and Viking settlements, as well as a medieval farm. There is also a 16th-century Laird's House, once home of the Earls Robert and Patrick Stewart.

**Open Apr-Sep, daily 9.30-18.30.**
Visitor centre with exhibition. Gift shop. Car and coach parking. Group concessions. &.
**Tel: 01950 460112**

# *Keills Chapel*

HS   NR 690806   LR: 55

*Off B8025, 6 miles SW of Tayvallich, Keills, Argyll.*

In the old chapel, which has been reroofed, is the Keills Cross, which is believed to date from the second half of the 8th century. Keills was an important ecclesiastical centre, and there is also a fine collection early Christian stones and carved grave slabs, most of them medieval. There are also early Christian stones housed in the reroofed chapel at Kilmory Knap [NR 702751], as well as a fine medieval cross and carved grave-slabs.

**Access at all reasonable times – short walk to chapel.**
Explanatory panels. Parking nearby.
**Tel: 0131 668 8800**
**Fax: 0131 668 8888**

# Kildalton Cross and Chapel

HS  NR 458508  LR: 60

*Off A846, 7 miles NE of Port Ellen,
Kildalton, Islay.*

The cross at Kildalton is the finest
surviving intact cross in Scotland, and
dates from the 8th century. The ringed
cross is carved from a single slab, and
bears the representation of the Virgin and
Child and angels on one side, while the
other has serpent and boss patterns with
four lions around the central boss. Other
representations illustrate biblical scenes.
The remains of a Viking ritual killing are
said to have been found beneath the
cross when it was excavated in 1890; and
there may have been an early Christian
community here. There is a medieval ruined chapel nearby, which houses
several carved grave slabs. The Thief's Cross, a 15th-century cross, also stands
nearby.

**Open all year.**
Parking nearby.
**Tel: 0131 668 8800   Fax: 0131 668 8888**

# Kilmartin House Museum

*On A816, 9 miles N of Lochgilphead, Kilmartin, Argyll.*

The museum has information about Dunadd and the people who lived in
Kilmartin Glen from earliest times, including burial cairns and standing stones.
There is an interesting audio-visual presentation and a museum which contains
artefacts and reconstructions.

**Open all year, daily 10.00-17.30.**
Guided tours by arrangement. Audio-visual and explanatory displays. Gift and
book shop. Cafe. WC. Disabled access and WC. Car parking. Group
concessions. ££.
**Tel: 01546 510278   Fax: 01546 510330**
**Web: www.kht.ork.uk**

# Kirkmadrine Early Christian Stones

HS   NX 080483   LR: 82

*Off A716, S of Sandhead, Kirkmadrine, Dumfries and Galloway.*

Displayed in the porch of the modern chapel are the oldest Christian monuments in Scotland outside Whithorn. A pillar stone, dating from the 5th century, is carved with a circled cross and Latin inscription 'Here lie the holy and chief priests, Ides, Viventius and Mavorius'. The two other 5th-century stones are also inscribed.

**Open all year.**
Disabled access. Parking nearby.
**Tel: 0131 668 8800   Fax: 0131 668 8888**

# Lumphanan

NO 578053   LR: 37

*Off A93, 5 miles NE of Aboyne, Lumphanan, Kincardine & Deeside.*

It was at Lumphanan that Macbeth was slain in battle by the forces of Malcolm in 1057. There is a large boulder – 'Macbeth's Stone' – at which he is said to have died [NJ 575034], and a well – 'Macbeth's Well' – where he drank before the battle [NJ 580039]. 'Macbeth's Cairn' [NJ 578053] is where he is believed to have been buried before his body was taken to Iona – although the robbed and disturbed cairn is actually a prehistoric burial cairn.

**Access at all reasonable times.**
Parking nearby.

# Macbeth Experience – Perthshire Visitor Centre, Bankfoot

NO 065353   LR: 53

*Off A9, 6 miles N of Perth, Bankfoot, Perthshire.*

The 'Macbeth Experience' is a multi-media audio-visual presentation which contrasts the wicked, murderous Macbeth of Shakespeare's play with the strong, able king of the 11th century.

**Open Apr-Sep, 9.00-20.00; Oct-Mar, 9.00-19.00.**

Audio-visual presentation. Gift shop. Restaurant. WC. Disabled access. Car and coach parking. Group concessions. £.
**Tel: 01738 787696**

# Meigle Sculptured Stone Museum

HS   NO 287447   LR: 53

*On A94, Meigle, Angus.*

A collection of 30 sculptured stones, one of the best collections of Dark Age sculpture in Western Europe. The stones were found at or near the old churchyard, and include the beautiful and remarkable Daniel Stone. A church is first said to have been established here by missionaries from Iona in 606. Meigle Parish Church is believed to be built in the site of this early foundation, and can be visited – check times locally. Meigle is also said to be the burial place of Guinevere, wife of Arthur.

   Less than one mile to the south-west is 'Macbeth's Stone', an eleven foot standing stone, which is decorated with scores of cup marks. It is said to mark the grave of a hero slain by Macbeth.

**Museum open Apr-Sep daily, 9.30-18.00; Oct-Nov, Mon-Sat 9.30-16.00, Sun 14.00-16.00.**
WC. Parking nearby. £.
**Tel: 01828 640612**

# Monymusk Church

NJ 685152   LR: 38

*Off B993, 6.5 miles SW of Inverurie, Aberdeenshire.*

Monymusk was a religious centre, and the Monymusk Reliquary, a casket which formerly contained the relics of St Columba, was long kept here. The Reliquary was carried before the Scottish army at the battle of Bannockburn in 1314, but is now kept in the Museum of Scotland. In the interesting church [NJ 685152] is a fine Pictish cross-slab.

**Open all year.**
Parking nearby.

# Mortlach Parish Church

NJ 323392   LR: 28

*Off A941, Dufftown, Moray.*

The present church, dedicated to St Moluag, dates from the 13th century, but stands on the site of an early Christian site. The Battle Stone, a Pictish symbol stone, survives in the interesting graveyard, and is decorated with sea monsters and beasts. There is another stone built into the entrance of the church.

**Open all year.**
Parking nearby.

# Netherton Cross, Hamilton

NS 723555   LR: 64

*Off A724, Strathmore Road, Hamilton Old Parish Church, Hamilton, Lanarkshire.*

Standing in the graveyard is the Netherton Cross, a 10th-century sculpted cross, decorated with figures, animals and cross-weave.

**Church open Mon-Fri, 10,30-15.30; other times by arrangement.**
Sales area. WC. Disabled access. Parking nearby.
**Tel: 01698 281905**

# Nith Bridge Cross Shaft, Thornhill

NX 868954   LR: 78

*Off A702, Thornhill, Dumfries and Galloway.*

The most complete Anglian Cross apart from Ruthwell, the cross shaft stands to about a height of nine feet: carvings include animals and winged beasts.

**Access at all reasonable times.**
Parking nearby.

# Paisley Abbey

NS 486640  LR: 64

*Off A737, Paisley, Renfrew.*

The Barrochan Cross, which dates from as early as the 8th century, is decorated with warriors and human figures. It is housed in the fine medieval abbey, which was dedicated to St Mirren. The church houses the stone effigy of Marjorie, daughter of Robert the Bruce; and the tomb of Robert II. The abbey is used as the parish church.

**Open all year: Mon-Sat 10.00-15.30.**
Refreshments. Sales area. WC. Limited disabled access. Parking nearby.
**Tel: 0141 889 7654**

# Ruthwell Cross

HS   NY 100682  LR: 85

*Off B724, 8.5 miles SE of Dumfries, Ruthwell, Dumfries and Galloway.*

A magnificent Anglian sculpted cross, dating from the 7th century, and standing some seventeen feet high. All four sides are decorated, the two wider sides with biblical scenes, while the other sides are carved with foliage and beasts. It was destroyed by the order of the General Assembly in 1640, but has since been reassembled from the broken pieces.

**Open all year – located in the parish church: key available from nearby.**
Parking.
**Tel: 0131 668 8800   Fax: 0131 668 8888**

# Scone Palace

NO 114267  LR: 58

*Off A93, N of Perth.*

Scone was a centre of the Picts and was also an ecclesiastical centre. The kings of Picts, then Scots from the reign of Kenneth I, were inaugurated at the Moot Hill, near the present palace. The Stone of Destiny, also called the Stone of Scone, was kept here, until taken to Westminster Abbey by Edward I in 1296 – although it was returned to Scotland in 1996, and is kept along with the Crown

Jewels in Edinburgh Castle. The last king to be inaugurated here was Charles I in 1651.

Scone Palace is a fine castellated mansion, which dates from 1802 and is built on the site of a medieval abbey.

***Open Good Friday-4th Mon Oct daily 9.30-17.15; last admission 16.45; other times by appt.***
Fine collections of furniture, clocks, needlework and porcelain. Gift shops. Restaurant. Tea-room. WC. Picnic area. 100 acres of wild gardens. Maze. Adventure playground. Meetings and conferences. Disabled access to state rooms & restaurant. Car and coach parking. Group concessions. £££.
**Tel: 01738 552300   Fax: 01738 552588**
**Email: SCONEPALACE@CQM.CO.UK**

# *St Andrews Cathedral*

HS   NO 516166   LR: 59

*Off A91, St Andrews, Fife.*

St Rule, a disciple of St Columba, founded a monastery at Kinrymont – St Andrews – in the 6th century, bringing with him the relics of St Andrew. An alternative version is that the relics of were brought here in 733 by Acca, bishop of Hexham. The bishopric was transferred from Abernethy in 908, and in the 12th century the Augustinian Order gradually displaced the Celtic monks. The church of the time – the tower of which, St Rule's Tower, still survives and dates from as early as 1070 – was too small so a large new cathedral was begun. The building was consecrated in 1318, but had to be rebuilt after a fire in 1380. After the Reformation the buildings fell into disuse and many were demolished.

The museum houses a large collection of Christian and early medieval sculpture, including cross-slabs, effigies, and other relics. St Rule's Tower is open to the public – magnificent views from the top. The castle is nearby.

***[Museum and St Rule's Tower] Open all year: Apr-Sep daily 9.30-18.30; Oct-Mar, daily 9.30-16.30; last ticket sold 30 mins before closing; closed 25/26 Dec & 1-3 Jan.***
Visitor centre with fine collection of Christian and early medieval sculpture, including cross-slabs, effigies, and other relics. Explanatory boards. Gift shop. Car parking nearby. Group concessions. £. Combined ticket for cathedral & castle is available (£).
**Tel: 01334 472563**

# St Blane's Church, Kingarth

HS  NS 094535  LR: 63

*Off A844, 2 miles S of Kingarth, Bute.*

Set in a scenic and quiet location are the remains of a Christian monastery of the 6th century. It was founded by St Blane, who came from Bute. The site is surrounded by an enclosure wall, and there are several ruinous structures, including 'The Cauldron', the purpose of which is unclear. There are the ruins of a fine 12th-century chapel, and an upper and lower burial yard, the upper part being used for men, while the

lower was for women. A spring here, reputedly a holy well (and also believed by some to be a wishing well) is known as St Blane's Well.
 Involves short walk.

***Access at all reasonable times.***
Parking nearby.
**Tel: 0131 668 8800   Fax: 0131 668 8888**

# St Ninian's Cave

HS  NX 421359  LR: 83

*Off A747, 4 miles SW of Whithorn, Physgill, Dumfries and Galloway.*

The cave, which is associated with St Ninian, has crosses carved into the walls.

***Access at all reasonable times – involves walk.***
**Tel: 0131 668 8800   Fax: 0131 668 8888**

# St Ronan's Church, Rona

HW 809323   LR: 8

*44 miles NE of Butt of Lewis, Rona.*

The complex of ruinous building forms one of the most complete groups of buildings from the early Celtic church in Scotland. There was a cell or hermitage here, dedicated to St Ronan, which dates from the 7th or 8th century. There are several cross-incised burial markers, dating from the 7th to 12th centuries. The island is accessible from Ness (in calm weather). It is a National Nature Reserve, in the care of Scottish National Heritage, from whom permission should be sought before visiting.

# St Vigeans Sculpted Stones

HS   NO 637430   LR: 83

*Off A933, 0.5 miles N of Arbroath, St Vigeans, Angus.*

A magnificent collection of early Christian and Pictish stones, housed in cottages, including the St Drostan Stone: St Drostan was a nephew of St Columba and active among the Picts. The stone has an ogham inscription, as well as other carvings of beasts, men and symbols. The collection ranks among the best in the world. Nearby and standing on an hillock is St Vigeans Church, which dates from the 12th century and is dedicated to St Vigean, a saint from Ireland who died in 664.

***Open daily Apr-Sep, 9.00-18.30.***
Parking nearby.
**Tel: 0131 668 8800   Fax: 0131 668 8888**

# Sueno's Stone, Forres

HS   NJ 809653   LR: 27

*Off A96, on E edge of Forres, Moray.*

This twenty foot high stone was elaborately carved in the 9th or 10th centuries, with a sculptured cross on one side and groups of warriors on the other. The stone is now protected by a glass canopy.

**Open all year.**
Parking nearby.
**Tel: 0131 668 8800   Fax: 0131 668 8888**

# Tarbert Castle

NR 867687   LR: 62

*Off A8015, E of Tarbert, Argyll.*

There was a stronghold here of the Dalriadian Scots, which was taken and burnt at least once. Around 1098 Magnus Barelegs, king of Norway, had his longship taken across the isthmus here to symbolise his possession of the Isles: Magnus claimed all the Hebrides – in fact anything which he could sail his longboat round. The site was used for a medieval castle, which is now ruinous.

**Access by footpath beside old police station, opposite Fish Quay.**
Parking nearby.

# Traprain Law Fort

NT 581746   LR: 67

*Off A1, 2 miles SE of East Linton, Traprain Law, East Lothian. There is a car park on the north side of the hill and a footpath to the summit.*

The fort consists of two main ramparts, but a much of the north-east of the hill has been quarried away. Lothian was controlled from here by the Britons known as the Gododdin. In 600, the northern Britons from Strathclyde and Cumbria, led by the Gododdin, marched south but were heavily defeated at Catterick. A large collection of Late Roman silver was found during excavation of the summit: it is now in the Museum of Scotland.

**Access at all reasonable times.**
Parking nearby.

# *Urquhart Castle*

HS   NH 531286   LR: 26

*Off A82, 1.5 miles E of Drumnadrochit, Highland.*

Standing in a picturesque location on the shore of Loch Ness, Urquhart is the site of a Pictish fort, which is believed to have existed here in the 6th century, which St Columba may have visited. St Columba is said to have confronted a beastie or kelpie in the loch – the first mention of a monster here. There have been many sightings of the Loch Ness Monster from near the castle – and there are two monster exhibition centres in nearby Drumnadrochit.

**Open all year – walk to castle: Apr-Sep daily 9.30-6.30; Oct-Mar daily 9.30-4.30; last entry 45 mins before closing; closed 25/26 Dec & 1/2 Jan.**
Gift shop. WC. Car and coach parking nearby. Group concessions. ££.
**Tel: 01456 450551**

# *Vikingar*

*Greenock Road, Largs, Ayrshire.*

The history of the Vikings in Scotland, from the first raids in Scotland to the battle of Largs in 1263, is told using multi-media techniques, including sight, sounds and smells.

**Open all year: Apr-Sep, 10.30-18.00; Oct-Mar, 10.30-16.00.**
Guided tours. Multimedia exhibition. Gift shop. Cafe and bar. Swimming pool and play area. WC. Full disabled access. Car and coach parking. Group concessions. ££.
**Tel: 01475 689777   Fax: 01475 689444**

# *Whithorn Priory*

HS   NX 444403   LR: 83

*On A746, Whithorn, Dumfries & Galloway. Joint ticket with Whithorn Priory and Museum.*

The site of the 5th-century Christian community of St Ninian, who built a stone church here, dedicated to St Martin of Tours. The church was white washed and known as 'Candida Casa' – White House – and its location was probably within the present ruined church. Nothing definite remains from this period except carved stones. Whithorn was a Northumbrian bishopric but is last mentioned in 803. The site was reused as a medieval priory, and was a place of pilgrimage. A fine collection of early Christian sculpture is housed in the nearby museum, including the Latinus Stone, the earliest Christian memorial in Scotland; the St Peter's Stone; and the 10th-century Monreith Cross, which is carved with interlaced patterns and has a round head. The Whithorn Trust Discovery Centre is also worth a visit. Joint ticket available.

***Site open all year; museum and centre open Easter-Oct 10.30-17.00.***
Site: Explanatory boards. Disabled access. Car and coach parking. Museum (£).
**Tel: 01988 500700**
Discovery Centre: Exhibition. Gift shop. Picnic area. WC. Car and coach parking.
Disabled access. Group concessions. £.
**Tel: 01988 500508**

*The Maiden Stone: a Pictish carved stone*

# Other Places of Interest

## Aberdeen Anthropological Museum

*Marischal College, Broad Street, Aberdeen.*

The museum exhibits several Pictish stones and artefacts from across Scotland, including the Goose, Collace and Fairy Green Stones.

**Open all year: Mon-Fri 10.00-17.00, Sun 14.00-17.00.**
Sales area. Temporary exhibitions. WC. Parties welcome but must book. Parking nearby.
**Tel: 01224 274301**

## Alyth Castle

NO 247485   LR: 53
*Off B954, 5 miles E of Blairgowrie and Rattray, Alyth, Perthshire.*

Guinevere, wife of King Arthur, was reputedly imprisoned here by the Picts. The site was later reused as a medieval castle. There is a Pictish cross-slab in the vestibule of the church in Alyth village [NO 243488].

**Open all year.**
Parking nearby.

## Antonine Wall

HS   NS 835798-NS 845799   LR: 65
*Off A803, E of Bonnybridge, Falkirk.*

The Antonine Wall, stretching from Bo'ness on the Forth to Old Kilpatrick on the Clyde, was built about 142-3 AD. It consisted of a turf rampart behind a ditch, with forts every two miles or so, and was not occupied for long: it was probably abandoned around 163 AD, although intermittently occupied in later campaigns. Remains are best preserved in the Falkirk/Bonnybridge area at Rough Castle [NS 835798-NS 845799]. There are some remains at the following: Bar Hill Fort, Bearsden Bathhouse, Castlecary, Croy Hill, Dullater, Seabegs Wood, Tollpark and Garnhall, and Watling Lodge.

Considered to be the best surviving visible Roman building in Scotland, the remains of Bearsden Bathhouse [NS 546720] were discovered in 1973 during excavations for a construction site.

***Access at all reasonable times.***
Explanatory board. Limited car parking.
**Tel: 0131 668 8800   Fax: 0131 668 8888**

# Hunterian Museum

*University of Glasgow, Glasgow.*

The museum covers geology, archaeology, coins and anthropology.

***Open all year: Mon-Sat 9.30-17.00; closed certain Public Holidays: phone to confirm.***
Gift shop. Cafe. WC. Parking nearby.
**Tel: 0141 330 4221   Fax: 0141 330 3617**

# Inverness Museum and Art Gallery

*Castle Wynd, Inverness.*

The museum also houses an excellent collection of Pictish artefacts and displays, including the beautiful Ardross Wolf and Deer.

***Open all year: Mon-Sat 9.00-17.00; closed public hols.***
Exhibitions. Gift shop. Restaurant. WC. Disabled access. Parking nearby.
**Tel: 01463 237114   Fax: 01463 225293**

# Museum nan Eilean, Stornoway

*Francis Street, Stornoway, Lewis.*

The museum holds collections illustrating life in the area from earliest times, including archaeology, history, domestic life and agriculture.

***Open all year: Apr-Sep, Mon-Sat 10.00-17.30; Oct-Nov, Thu-Fri 10.00-17.00, Sat 10.00-13.00.***
Exhibitions. WC. Limited disabled access. Parking nearby.
**Tel: 01851 703773 x266   Fax: 01851 706318**
**Email: rlanghome@w-isles.gov.uk**

# Museum of Scotland

*Chambers Street, Edinburgh.*

This magnificent new museum houses extensive collections, covering all aspects of Scotland.

**Open all year Mon-Sat 10.00-17.00, Sun 12.00-17.00; closed 25/26 Dec & 1/2 Jan.**
Museum. Gift shop. Audio guides. Tea-rooms. WC. Disabled access & WC. Parking nearby.
**Tel: 0131 225 7534   Fax: 0131 220 4819**

# Orkney Museum

*Tankerness House, Broad Street, Kirkwall, Orkney*

One of the finest vernacular town houses in Scotland, this 16th-century building now contains a museum of Orkney history, including the islands' fascinating archaeology. The museum contains several stones and artefacts from the Pictish era, excavated from all over the Orkney islands.

**Open all year: Apr-Sep, Mon-Sat 10.30-17.00 (May-Sep, Sun 14.00-17.00); Oct-Mar, Mon-Sat 10.30-12.30 & 13.30-17.00.**
Guided tours by arrangement. Exhibitions. Gift shop. Garden. WC. Disabled access. Parking nearby.
**Tel: 01856 873191   Fax: 01856 871560**

# Perth Museum and Art Gallery

*George Street, Perth.*

This purpose-built museum houses fine collections on history and archaeology, as well as Pictish stones including the St Madoe's cross-slab.

**Open all year Mon-Sat 10.00-17.00; closed Christmas & New Year.**
Exhibitions. Gift shop. WC. Disabled access. Car parking.
**Tel: 01738 632488   Fax: 01738 443505**

# Shetland Museum

*Lower Hillhead, Lerwick, Shetland.*

The museum has a fascinating range of items and houses a permanent collection of artefacts, models, displays and specimens which illustrate the story of Shetland from prehistoric times until the present day. Exhibits include replicas of the St Ninian's Isle treasure (which was snaffled by the Museum of Scotland), as well as sculpted stones including the Mail figure, with a wolf-headed man, and the Monk's Stone, an early cross-slab.

**Open all year: Mon, Wed & Fri 10.00-19.00; Tue, Thu & Sat, 10.00-17.00.**
Exhibitions. Gift shop. WC. Disabled access (lift) and WC. Parking nearby.
**Tel: 01595 695057   Fax: 01595 696729**

The following sites in England are also open to the public: Hadrians's Wall; the impressive forts at Housesteads and Chesters; Hexham Abbey; Lindisfarne Priory; Bamburgh Castle; Alnwick Castle; Durham Cathedral; and the site of the Synod of Whitby at Whitby Abbey in Yorkshire. Also the Yorvick Centre in York.

*Alnwick Castle*

# *Index*

Abercorn, 24, 26, 46
Aberdeen, 81
Aberlemno, 14, 25, 46
Abernethy, 13, 31, 47, 49
Acca, 20, 27, 75
Adamnan, 19, 20, 63
Adrian, St, 32
Aed, son of Eochaid, d 777, 27
Aed, son of Kenneth I, d 878, 32, 33
Aedan, son of Gabhran, 20, 22, 54
Aidan, St, 21
Alexander, son of Malcolm III, 41
Alnwick, 41, 84
Alpin d 834, 31
Alyth Castle, 81
Andrew, St, 20, 27, 75
Angles, 9, 15, 18, 21, 22, 24, 25, 27, 48, 60
Angus I, son of Fergus, d 761, 26, 27
Angus II, son of Fergus, d 854, 30
Antonine Wall, 12, 81-82
Applecross, 21, 47-48
Athelstan, king of Wessex, 35, 36, 58
Auld Kirk of Kilbirnie, 48
Baldred, St, 27, 48
Bamburgh, 18, 34, 84
Banquo, 7, 8, 63
Barr, St, 17, 51
Bass Rock, 27, 48
Bernicia see Northumberland
Bethoc, daughter of Malcolm II, 39
Birnam Wood, 57, 59
Blane, St, 20, 55, 76
Boece, Hector, 5, 6, 7
Bower, Walter, 5
Brunanburgh, battle of, 35
Brechin Cathedral, 47, 49
Brendan, St, 18, 48, 61
Britons, 9, 13, 14, 15, 17, 18, 20, 22, 24, 27, 30, 32, 35, 37, 52, 60, 78
Brough of Birsay, 40, 49
Brude, son of Bile, d 693, 24, 25, 26, 46
Brude, son of Feredach d 843, 31
Brude, son of Maelchon, d 584, 19, 22
Burghead, 7, 13, 40, 50
Caledonians, 11, 12, 13
Calgacus, 11
Canute see Cnut
Carham, battle of, 39, 53, 60
Carlisle, 15
Cathedral of St Moluag, Lismore, 20, 50
Catterick, 22, 78
Cawdor Castle, 8, 40, 51
Cellach, abbot of Iona, 29
Cellach, bishop of St Andrews, 35

Ceretic, king of Strathclyde, 18
Cille Bharra, 51-52
Cnut, king of England, 7, 39
Cormac, St, 20, 61
Columba, St, 5, 18, 19, 20, 22, 30, 35, 50, 54, 57, 61, 67, 72, 75, 79
Constantine I, son of Kenneth I, d 879, 32, 33
Constantine II, son of Aed, d 952, 6, 34, 35
Constantine III, son of Aed, d 997, 38
Constantine, son of Fergus, d 820, 29, 30
Corbridge, battles of, 34, 35
Cowie, 36
Craig Phaidraig, 18
Crinan, bishop of Dunkeld, d 1045, 7, 39, 40
Cruithne, 14
Cruithni, 13
Cul Drebane, battle of, 18
Culen, son of Indulf, d 971, 37
Cullen, 36
Culross, 20, 52
Cumbria, 14, 78
Cupar Castle, 8, 52
Cuthbert, St, 21, 39
Dalriada/Dal Riata, 14, 15, 18, 20, 21, 22, 23, 24, 25, 26, 27, 29, 30, 31, 32, 54, 55, 58, 60, 66
David, son of Malcolm Canmore, 41
Deer, 19, 53
Degastan, 22
Dollar, 32
Donald Breac, son of Eochaid, d 642, 23, 24
Donald I, son of Alpin, d 863, 32
Donald II, son of Constantine I, d 900, 33, 41, 58
Donald, son of Aed, d 916, 34
Donada, daughter of Malcolm II, 7, 40
Drest, 23, 24
Drostan, St, 19, 53, 77
Duff, son of Malcolm I, d 967, 37, 63
Dufftown, 39
Dumbarton, 15, 27, 32, 53
Dunadd, 15, 20, 25, 26, 31, 54, 60, 70
Dunaverty, 15, 54-55
Dunbar, 31, 35
Dunblane Cathedral, 55
Dunimarle Castle, 8, 52, 57
Dunkeld, 13, 29, 30, 31, 34, 35, 57
Dunnichen see Nechtansmere
Dunnottar, 33, 35, 58

Dunollie, 15, 58
Dunsinane Hill, 8, 40, 57, 59
Dunstaffnage, 15, 59-60
Durham, 21, 39, 40, 84
Eadalf of Northumberland, 39
Eadbehrt of Northumberland, 27
Eadred, king of Wessex, 36
Ealdred of Northumberland, 34, 35
Eanfrith, 23
Ecgfrith, 24, 25
Edgar, king of England, 37
Edgar, son of Malcolm Canmore, 41
Edinburgh, 14, 15, 23, 36, 41, 60
Edmund , king of Wessex, 36
Edmund, son of Malcolm III, 41
Edward, son of Malcolm III, 41
Edward the Elder, 35
Edwin, 23
Eileach an Naoimh, 61
Eilean Mor, South Knapdale, 20, 61
Elgin, 6, 40, 50, 61-62
Enoch, St, 20, 52
Eochaid, son of Rhun d 889, 32, 33
Eric Bloodaxe, 35, 36
Ethelfrith, 22, 23
Ethelred II of England, 37, 38
Ethelred, son of Malcolm III, 41
Fergus, son of Erc, d 500, 5, 18, 31
Fettercairn, 37
Fetteresso, 36
Fillan, St, 27
Finella, 37, 62
Finella's Castle, 37, 62
Finlay, mormaer of Moray, 40
Fleance, 8
Fordoun, 36
Fordoun, John of, 5
Forres, 33, 37, 39, 63
Forteviot, 13, 31, 32, 63
Fortingall, 63
Galloway, 11, 14, 17, 27, 31
Garvallachs, 18
Giric, son of Donald, d 889, 32, 33, 56
Giric, son of Kenneth III, d 1005, 7, 38
Glamis Castle, 8, 40, 64
Glasgow, 20, 52, 64-65
Glendochart, 27
Glenelg, 10
Gododdin, 15, 22, 78
Govan Old Parish Church, 65
Green Castle see Finella's Castle
Groam House Museum and Pictish Centre, Rosemarkie, 14, 65
Gruoch, granddaughter of Kenneth III, 7, 9, 40
Gurness Broch, 66
Guthrum, 33
Hadrian (and wall), 12, 17, 84
Harold, king of England, 40, 41
Hastings, battle of, 40, 41
Hebrides, 7, 9, 14, 15, 20, 29, 30, 40

Hexham, 21, 84
Holinshed, 6
Holy Island, 21, 66
Hunterian Museum, 82
Ida of Northumberland, 18
Inchinnan Early Christian Stones, 67
Inchtuthill, 12
Indulf, son of Constantine II, 36, 37
Ingibiorg, daughter of Thorfinn, 40, 41
Inveresk, 12
Inverness, 13, 67, 40, 82
Iona, 18, 20, 24, 27, 29, 67, 68
Ireland, 23, 24, 39, 54
Ivar, king of Dublin, 32, 34
James VI, 5
Jarlshof, 69
Julius Agricola, 11
Julius Caesar, 11
Keills Chapel, 69
Kells, Book of, 20, 27, 29
Kenneth I (MacAlpin), son of Alpin, d 859, 5, 30, 31, 32, 54, 63, 74
Kenneth II, son of Malcolm, d 995, 37
Kenneth III d 1005, 7, 38, 62
Kentigern *see* Mungo
Kildalton Cross and Chapel, 70
Kilmartin House Museum, 70
Kinrymont *see* St Andrews
Kirkmadrine, 18, 71
Kyle, 27
Lindisfarne, 21, 22, 29, 84
Lismore, 20, 50
Loch Ness, 19, 79
Lothian, 14, 23, 24, 27, 34, 36, 38, 39, 60, 78
Lulach the Fool, 9, 40
Lumphanan, 9, 40, 59, 71
Luncarty, battle of, 38
Macbeth d 1057, 5, 6, 7, 8, 9, 20, 40, 50, 51, 52, 59, 61, 63, 64, 67, 68, 71, 72
Macbeth's Castle, Dunsinane, 59
Macbeth's Castle, Inverness, 67
Macbeth Experience - Perthshire Visitor Centre, Bankfoot, 71-72
Macbeth's Hillock, 63
Macbeth's Law, 59
Macbeth's Stone, Cairn and Well, Lumphannan, 71
Macbeth's Stone, Meigle, 72
MacDuff, Lady, 7, 8, 52, 57
Machrie Moor, 10
Maeatae, 13
Maelchon
Maelrubha, St, 21, 47
Maes Howe, 10
Malcolm I, son of Donald, 35, 36
Malcolm II, son of Kenneth II, 6, 38, 39, 64
Malcolm III Canmore, d 1093, 5, 7, 8, 9, 40, 41, 57, 59, 67, 71

Malcolm, son of Donald, king of Strathclyde d 997, 37, 38
Malcolm Canmore's Tower, Pittencrieff Park, 57
Manaw, 26
Margaret, wife of Malcolm Canmore, 41, 56, 60, 68
May, Isle of, 32
Meigle Sculptured Stone Museum, 14, 72
Melrose, 21, 31
Molaise, St, 21, 66
Moluag, St, 20, 50, 73
Monan, St, 32
Mons Graupius, 11
Monymusk Church, 72-73
Monymusk Reliquary, 72-73
Monzievaird, 38
Moot Hill, Scone, 31, 74
Mortlach, 20, 73
Mousa, 10
Mungo, St, 20, 52, 64-65
Museum nan Eilean, Stornoway, 82
Museum of Scotland, 14, 27, 47, 49, 50, 52, 73, 78, 83
Nechtan, son of Derile, 26
Nechtansmere, 25, 26, 46
Netherton Cross, Hamilton, 73
Newstead, 12
Ninian, St, 17, 76, 79
Nith Bridge Cross Shaft, Thornhill, 73
Norsemen *see* Vikings
Northumbria, 7, 18, 21, 22, 23, 24, 25, 26, 27, 31, 32, 33, 34, 35, 36, 46, 53, 60
Novantae, 14
Olaf Gothfrithsson, 35
Olaf the White, king of Dublin, 32
Orkney, 7, 9, 14, 24, 29, 30, 39, 40, 83
Oswald, 23
Oswiu d 670, 23, 24
Owen, king of Strathclyde fl 642, 24
Owen, son of Donald, king of Strathclyde, d 937, 34, 35
Owen the Bald, king of Strathclyde d 1018, 39, 53
Paisley Abbey, 74
Patrick, St, 17, 18
Perth, 83
Picts, 9, 12, 13, 14, 17, 19, 22, 23, 24, 25, 26, 27, 29, 30, 31, 46, 47, 49, 50, 53, 54, 55, 56, 57, 58, 62, 63, 66, 67, 69, 73, 74, 77, 79, 81, 82, 83
Pontius Pilate, 63
Quoyness, 10
Rheged, 22, 24
Rhiderch Hen, 22
Rhiderch, son of Donald of Strathclyde, 37
Rhun d 872, 32
Rognvald, 34, 35

Romans, 11, 12, 13, 14, 15, 17
Rosemarkie, 14, 20, 65
Rule, St, 17, 20, 27, 75
Ruthwell Cross, 24, 74
Saxons, 12, 15
Scythia, 13
Scone, 13, 31, 32, 54, 60, 74-75
Scots, 9, 12, 13, 14, 15, 18, 23, 26, 27, 32, 33, 34, 35, 38, 53, 54, 58, 74, 78
Serf, St, 20, 46, 52, 60
Shakespeare, 5, 7, 40
Shetland, 9, 14, 29, 30, 39, 40, 84
Sigurd the Mighty, earl of Orkney, 33
Sigurd the Stout, earl of Orkney, 7, 39
Siward of Northumberland, 8
St Andrews, 20, 27, 35, 37, 75
St Blane's Church, Kingarth, 76
St Ninian's Cave, 18, 76
St Ronan's Church, Rona, 77
St Vigeans Sculpted Stones, 14, 77
Stainmore, 36, 37
Strathearn, 34
Street of the Dead, 68
Stone of Destiny/Scone, 18, 20, 31, 54, 60, 74
Strathcarron, battle of, 24
Strathclyde, 14, 15, 22, 24, 27, 30, 33, 34, 35, 37, 38, 39, 52, 53, 78
Sueno's Stone, Forres, 78
Tacitus, 11
Tarbert, 15, 78
Tarlorgen, son of Eanfrith, d 657, 23
Theneu, St *see* Enoch, St
Thorfinn the Mighty, earl of Orkney, 7, 9, 39, 40, 49, 50
Thorsten the Red, 32
Traprain Law Fort, 15, 78
Trumwin, bishop of Abercorn, 24, 46
Tyningham, 27, 35, 48
Uhtred of Northumbria, 37, 39
Urien, d 590, 22
Urquhart, 13, 19, 79
Votadini *see* Gododdin
Whitby, Synod of, 24, 84
Whithorn, 17, 18, 71, 79-80
William the Conquerer, 40, 41
York, 35, 36, 84